The Amateurs' Guide to
Leisuretime Photography

SUZANNE BEEDELL

The Amateurs' Guide to Leisuretime Photography

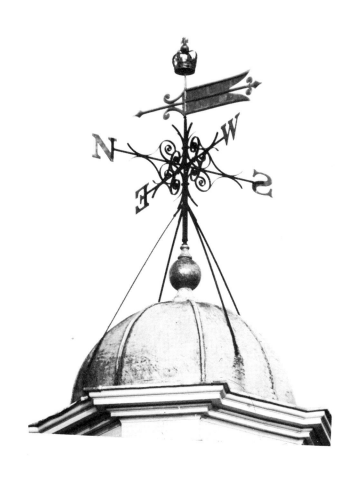

John Bartholomew and Son Ltd
Edinburgh

First published in Great Britain 1975
by John Bartholomew & Son Ltd,
12 Duncan Street, Edinburgh EH9 1TA
and at 216 High Street, Bromley BR1 1PW

Printed in Belgium by "Les Presses Saint-Augustin", Bruges
SBN 0 7028 1001 0

CONTENTS

DEDICATION

To my daughters Jane and Catherine, and to my new grandson.
I hope they will, in the future, look back on all my photographs as a record of their youth and times remembered.

ACKNOWLEDGMENTS

My grateful thanks to Ginette Leach who has helped with
research, done most of the typing, and spent hours in the
darkroom helping with the photographs, in spite of loathing
that particular job.

Introduction

As a writer on practical subjects, I realised years ago that it was much easier to get on with my work if I could illustrate my own books, and also that it paid me. Of course this was a wonderful excuse for me to buy cameras and equipment and indulge in a hobby which has fascinated me from childhood.

I owned my first Box Brownie when I was nine; I used a Vest Pocket Kodak—a wonderful little folding camera—and eventually a Voigtlander folding camera of my own. With all those cameras I struggled to take photographs like those in photographic books and magazines, taken with expensive Zeiss, Contax, Leicas and Kodaks which were then every amateur photographer's dream. I had neither the knowledge, the technique, nor the equipment, although I did have the beginnings of an eye, and I achieved a few good family snapshots. Then came colour transparency film, and eventually I graduated to 35mm miniature cameras, changing several times for more expensive and refined models, and buying extra lenses and equipment on the way, until I now have all the equipment I need, or at any rate can justify. My basic 35mm camera cost less than £200—not all that expensive really, just in the middle of the range—and my twin lens reflex was a lot cheaper than that. But I am not a professional photographer in the sense that photography is my entire living, and I am not rich, so I can afford only the equipment that is strictly necessary to enable me to take colour and black and white photographs for pleasure and for reproduction. So I can equate my own experience with that of anyone who is seriously trying to take better pictures, and who enjoys photographs as a hobby, and would make a bit of money out of it if he could, and who can afford to spend some money on it.

There are many books about photography which go far more deeply into the subject than I have room for here. Photography consists of three processes. The taking, the developing, and the printing of the picture. At all stages one has control over, and can alter, the final result. But for most of us the taking is the thing. To set up a dark room and learn the techniques of controlling film development is more than we want to do—we rely on the professional photographic laboratory to process our film. Most processors are amenable to requests to develop a whole film for contrast or softness, but not to process each frame individually. The printing of a photograph is vitally important, yet it requires only an enlarger and a very basic dark room—a blacked-out bathroom or kitchen will do. To achieve any sort of standard of prints it is necessary to do this for yourself.

This page.
Left: Major automatic print washer.
Right: A smaller Standard automatic print washer.

Facing page.
Top: Paterson 'system 4' Developing tanks, the largest shown holds 5 rolls of film.

Facing page.
Bottom: A contact proof printer.

The equipment illustrated gives an added refinement to the dark room, but it is not essential.

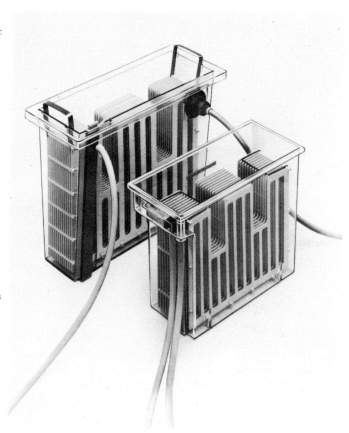

This book is intended to help you to take good pictures of your leisure activities, with just a reasonable amount of basic equipment. Pictures that can be satisfactorily processed without speciality work being necessary, and pictures that will, photographically and artistically, reach standards high enough to satisfy all but the complete purist.

Too many photographic books rattle on about the slight technical faults of pictures that seem, as pictures, to be perfectly good enough to you and me. Faults that might prevent them from winning competitions judged by other photographers, are of little importance to the novice whose main concern is the content of the picture itself. What "experts" often forget when judging any art form is that technique does not replace artistic talent; it merely supplements it; and that subjects which he—because so many people have made photographs of them—describes as "trite" may seem very beautiful indeed to the less blasé amateur.

So this book will describe basic equipment, and then go on to talk about taking pictures of different leisure activities under differing circumstances, and in the process all kinds of technical matters will come up and be dealt with simply. Always keeping in mind that the picture is the thing. Whether you are recording a memorable holiday or a sporting occasion or sporting technique, or making a record of your hobby, or a collection of photographs of your pet subject, it is pictures, not snapshots, that you are after. A snapshot is of interest only to the taker and the subject, but a picture is of interest to complete strangers.

Plate 1 and 1a:
Ordinary but beautiful subjects, taken on medium-speed film, ASA 125:
f. 11 at 1/250 second.

Kodak pocket
'Instamatic 50'
camera.

Kodak pocket
'Instamatic 300'
camera with
'magicube' and
'magicube' extender.

CHAPTER 1   Cameras

Unless you have at least a little talent for it you can own the best cameras and equipment that money can buy and still never take a picture that anyone but yourself will look at twice. Yet there is no doubt that if you can take pictures, and have some technical know-how about photography, the better your equipment the better your pictures will be.

The cheaper and less complex cameras can produce absolutely first-class pictures, provided they are used within their limitations of lighting conditions and range. The simplest cameras have lenses pre-set to take sharp pictures of things from about 7ft (2 metres) from the camera to infinity, in good light conditions, and are useless for close-up work without extra lenses (occasionally obtainable) and have shutters pre-set at only one or two speeds, so are useless for fast-moving subjects. As the price goes up, so does the complexity and adaptability of the camera, and you can photograph a wider range of subjects in widely-differing lighting conditions. Go more expensive still, and whole sets of interchangeable lenses and extra refinements of viewfinding, focusing and setting become available for each camera, giving the photographer a tremendous amount of range and control.

Simple cameras often have magazine loading.

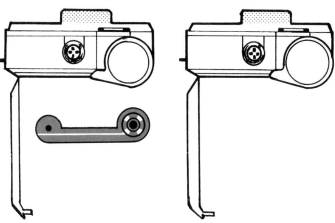

Because in advanced cameras the complexities of exposure and focusing become harder to understand and master when you are trying to decide very quickly how to set the camera, manufacturers have gone to great lengths to make completely automatic cameras with all the refinements. Point one of these cameras at the subject and it sets itself with just a little help from the photographer. This ensures perfect exposures every time through high-quality lenses, and is splendid for the photographer who is not after special effects, and does not understand his camera. But special conditions do arise and special effects are wanted sooner or later, so these clever automatic cameras can also be set manually, just like those without automatic controls.

Photographers are rarely satisfied with their cameras, and always long to get that better one or those extra lenses, but it is a mistake to start by buying highly-expensive gear that you do not know how to use.

So get a cheap pre-set miniature camera for snapshotting only, but if you are a beginner who wishes to start with something on which you can cut your photographic teeth and learn some of the technicalities, go for a medium-price-range camera. Having mastered that, you will probably want to change it for a more expensive camera with interchangeable lenses and more flexibility, until you finally achieve something that does everything you want of it. At this later stage make sure the camera you buy does have a set of lenses and accessories available, so that you can build up on it as you want to. There is nothing more annoying than to buy a camera which is fine at first, only to discover later that it

Below: A direct vision miniature camera.

Below right: A pocket camera with 2 shutter speeds, and a built in flashcube system. The action of opening the camera cocks the shutter and transports the film.

cannot be fitted with interchangeable lenses. Luckily, cameras, like cars, have a secondhand value, and most dealers will take an old camera in part exchange for a new one, although of course you are bound to drop a bit of money!

The next consideration is the type of picture you intend to take. Although all cameras will take both black-and-white and colour pictures on a variety of films there are some variables to consider. First of all, if you want to take colour transparencies for home viewing, then the size of the picture produced by the camera is vital, as the slides must not exceed the size that fits standard home projectors. These normally take a plastic or cardboard or glass slide 50 millimetres square. The picture held in this slide is usually 24 × 36mm, but can vary from about 40mm square to 28mm × 28mm, 12mm × 17mm, or 8mm × 11mm. There are cameras available which take only 8mm × 11mm and 12mm × 17mm or 28mm × 27mm, but standard 35mm miniature cameras, already described in this chapter, take pictures 24mm × 36mm. Some of the larger format cameras can have masks inserted in the back to reduce the size of each frame to fit standard slides.

Another popular type of camera is the twin lens reflex, taking pictures 56 mm × 56 mm, too big for the standard projector, although special projectors can be bought with slide holders of this size.

Miniature cameras take 20 or 36 pictures per roll or cassette of film. Twin-lens reflex take 12. This is an advantage if for a specific purpose only a dozen pictures are needed, not 20 or 36. Perhaps you have taken a dozen pictures of an important game, and want to see them quickly. You don't want to waste the rest of a 35 mm film, or to have to shut yourself in a cupboard to open the camera and cut and reload the film, all by feel in pitch darkness.

On the other hand, the actual *area* of film in one roll for the big camera is not all that different from the area of a 35 mm film, so it will not cost appreciably less for 12 exposures on 120 film than it does for 36 exposures on 35 mm film. This is an important factor when using expensive colour film. 12 large transparencies cost almost as much as 36 small ones.

The 35 mm and smaller format cameras are also fine for black and white photography, but if you are going for really top class black-and-whites, or for colour photography for reproduction, then the larger format camera will produce better work. Especially black-and-white pictures, because normally one intends to enlarge all or part of the negative, and the bigger the enlargement of any negative the poorer the definition will be. Obviously the degree of enlargement required to produce a half-plate picture from a 35 mm negative will be much greater than that required to produce a half-plate picture from a 56 mm negative.

If you want to take pictures of fast-moving objects a miniature camera is much easier to use. The camera is held to the eye and the object is seen directly through the view-finder, so that it is almost automatic to swing the camera as if it were part of your head. Because for technical reasons the picture you see on the viewing screen of a twin lens reflex camera held at waist level moves across the screen in the opposite direction to that in which you are swinging the camera, your brain tells you that you are swinging it the wrong way, and it is quite difficult to train yourself to ignore this signal. It is rather like trying to make a circular movement with one hand and a straight movement with the other hand at

A pocket camera with electronically controlled shutter and infinitely variable exposure times between 15 seconds and 1/500 second. Apertures between f/2.8 and f/22.

the same moment. Of course, when photographing still subjects this problem does not arise, and the ease with which you can see, focus, and compose a picture in the big viewing screen of the twin lens reflex is one factor in its favour, and in this respect it is much easier for a beginner to use.

The better miniature cameras have interchangeable lenses, from very wide angle to enormous telephoto, enabling the photographer to take pictures from close to an object and still get all of it in (see Interchangeable Lenses), and from miles away and yet bring it so near that it appears to be just in front of the camera. Unfortunately few twin lens reflex cameras have a range of interchangeable lenses, and this can be a decisive factor when considering which camera to buy.

There are also problems with interchangeable lenses for miniature cameras. The more expensive cameras with focal plane shutters, which work in the camera body, and are just a pair of blinds, with a variable slot between them, which open and close across the film so that in the closed position no light can reach it, have interchangeable lenses, and the threads or bayonet mounts by which these fit into the camera body are standardised to some extent so that lenses of one make will fit cameras of another make. Thus, if you have a camera with a focal-plane shutter and standard thread or bayonet fittings

Below: A focal-plane shutter.

Below right: Between the lens shutter.

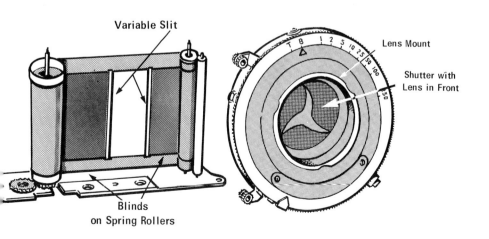

Variable Slit

Lens Mount

Shutter with Lens in Front

Blinds
on Spring Rollers

and change it for another focal-plane-shutter camera with the same standard fittings you can use the interchangeable lenses you already have, and will not have to buy a complete new set.

Cameras with between-the-lens shutters (usually a diaphragm that opens and shuts inside the lens itself) may not have interchangeable lenses, because to take out the lens and put in another one would mean that the film in the camera would be exposed to the light. Some makes have lenses in which only the front components are removed, leaving the shutter and back components of the lens in place, and differing supplementary front components are attached as required. This means that only the special lenses for that make of camera can be used.

There are specialist cameras for specialist work, and I shall mention them when the need arises in later sections of this book.

Cheap cameras do not have exposure meters either built into the camera body or working through the lenses. Medium price miniature cameras may have exposure meters built in on the camera body, and as the prices go up "through-the-lens" metering becomes standard. It usually takes the form of a needle actuated by a tiny battery and a special cell, which swings in the viewfinder against a printed scale, so that as you point the camera you can see if the exposure is going to be correct. In automatic cameras this needle actuates the exposure controls to pre-set the camera all by itself. In manual cameras the needle moves as you adjust the aperture and exposure settings. Without any kind of self-contained exposure meter you will have to guess at exposures or use a hand-held meter (page 33 exposure meters). A "through-the-lens" meter certainly makes life easy, and it is well worth spending extra money on a camera that has one.

Focussing and range finding are achieved by various systems, and again, the more expensive the camera the clearer and more exact they are likely to be. As stated above, the twin lens reflex uses a big screen, the same size as the eventual negative, on to which you look from above, the image being projected on to the screen from below via the viewing lens, which is coupled to the taking lens.

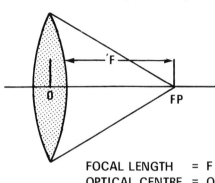

FOCAL LENGTH

**BUILT IN
EXPOSURE METER
NEEDLE AS SEEN
IN VIEWFINDER**

FOCAL LENGTH   = F
OPTICAL CENTRE = O
FOCAL POINT   = FP

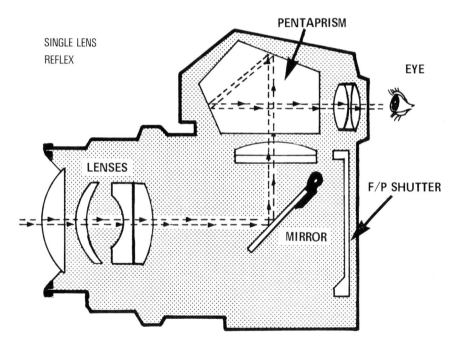

SINGLE LENS
REFLEX

PENTAPRISM

EYE

LENSES

F/P SHUTTER

MIRROR

The direct vision miniature camera has a viewfinder through which to look directly at the object, or in the case of the single lens reflex the image passes from the object through the single taking lens, through mirrors and prisms, to the eye.

SOME MINIATURE CAMERAS

Camera	Film Size	Format	Lens	Shutter	Meter	Manual Over-ride	Size
Kodak 100	110 (Special perf. 16mm)	13 × 17mm	25mm f/11 fixed focus	1/60	N/A	No	$4\frac{1}{2} \times 2 \times 1$in
Kodak 200	110 (Special perf. 16mm)	13 × 17mm	25mm f/11 fixed focus	1/80 & 1/40	N/A	No	$4\frac{1}{2} \times 2 \times 1$in
Kodak 300	110 (Special perf. 16mm)	13 × 17mm	26mm f/5.6 fixed focus	1/80 & 1/40	N/A	Manual operation	$4\frac{1}{2} \times 2 \times 1$in
Kodak 400	110 (Special perf. 16mm)	13 × 17mm	25mm f/11 fixed focus	1/300 to 20 secs	Auto	No	$5\frac{1}{8} \times 2 \times 1$in
Kodak 500	110 (Special perf. 16mm)	13 × 17mm	26mm f/5.6 fixed focus	1/300 to 20 secs	Auto	No	$5\frac{1}{8} \times 2 \times 1$in
Kodak 50	110 (Special perf. 16mm)	13 × 17mm	26mm f/2.7 "Ektar" focusing	1/250 to 5 secs	Auto	No	$5\frac{3}{4} \times 2\frac{1}{4} \times 1$in
Kodak 60	110 (Special perf. 16mm)	13 × 17mm	26mm f/2.7 "Ektar" focusing/ rangefinder	1/250 to 5 secs	Auto	No	$5\frac{3}{4} \times 2\frac{1}{4} \times 1$in
GAF 220	110 (Special perf. 16mm)	13 × 17mm	26.5mm f/9.5 fixed focus 3 elements	1/100 to 1/40 sec	N/A	No	$5 \times 2\frac{1}{8} \times 1\frac{1}{16}$in
GAF 440	110 (Special perf. 16mm)	13 × 17mm	27mm f/9 fixed focus	1/500 to 10 secs	Auto	No	$5 \times 2\frac{1}{8} \times 1\frac{1}{16}$in
Agfamatic 2000	110 (Special perf. 16mm)	13 × 17mm	26mm f/ Color Agnar lens	—	N/A	No	$4\frac{2}{5} \times 2\frac{1}{8} \times 1$in

Camera	Film	Frame size	Lens / Focusing	Shutter speeds	Metering		Dimensions
Minolta 16 MG-S	16mm (Single perf.)	12 × 17mm K	23mm f/2.8 "Rokkor" zone focusing	1/500 to 1/30 secs	Auto	No	$4\frac{1}{4} \times 1\frac{5}{16} \times 1\frac{1}{16}$ in
Minolta 16PS	16mm (Any)	10 × 14mm	25mm f/3.5 "Rokkor" fixed focusing	1/100 & 1/30	N/A	No	—
Yashica Atoron Electro	9.5mm (Unperf.)	8 × 11mm	18mm f/2.8 Yashica focusing	1/350 to 8 secs	Auto	No	$4\frac{1}{8} \times 1\frac{1}{2} \times \frac{3}{4}$ in
Minox B	9.5mm (Unperf.)	8 × 11mm	15mm f/3.5 "Complan" fixed aperture focusing	1/1000 to $\frac{1}{2}$ sec	Non auto coupled (Selenium)	Manual operation	$3\frac{7}{8} \times 1 \times \frac{3}{4}$ in
Minox BL	9.5mm (Unperf.)	8 × 11mm	15mm f/3.5 "Complan" fixed aperture focusing	1/1000 to $\frac{1}{2}$ sec	Non auto coupled (CdS)	Manual operation	$3\frac{15}{16} \times 1\frac{1}{8} \times \frac{5}{8}$ in
Minox C	9.5mm (Unperf.)	8 × 11mm	15mm f/3.5 "Complan" fixed aperture focusing	1/1000 to 7 secs	Auto	Yes	$4\frac{3}{4} \times 1 \times \frac{3}{4}$ in
Tessina 35L	35mm (Standard)	14 × 21mm	25mm f/2.8 focusing TLR	1/500 to $\frac{1}{2}$ sec	Non auto coupled	Manual operation	$2\frac{5}{8} \times 2 \times \frac{3}{4}$ in

As you turn the focussing ring of the miniature camera or the focussing knob of the twin lens reflex, the image on the viewfinder or on the screen moves in and out of focus. Some miniature cameras have a bright area, or a spot in which the focussing can be very clearly and exactly seen, or have a double image which disappears as the lens is focussed. Whichever kind of camera you buy, test it well and choose one you find easy to focus. For those with bad sight the twin lens reflex with

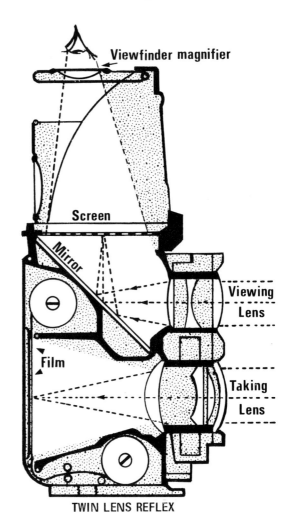

Viewfinder magnifier

Screen

Mirror

Viewing Lens

Film

Taking Lens

TWIN LENS REFLEX

focussing screen is much easier to use than the miniature camera with eye level viewfinder and focussing arrangements. Those who wear only reading glasses will not have too much of a problem with miniature cameras, but those whose long sight is bad and is heavily corrected by glasses are likely to be in trouble, although correcting lenses are obtainable for eye level viewfinders.

Having assessed all these factors as they apply to you, you should, with the assistance of a helpful and expert camera salesman, be able to make a good choice of camera. There are so many refinements and special features, differing in every make of camera, that it is impossible here to detail them all; it would take a whole book and we would never get to the photography! Makers claim that their own particular refinements are the best and new models are constantly being produced, so that it finally becomes very hard to decide which is best for you personally. Be comforted in that whatever the make of camera, and whatever the price, modern cameras are splendid pieces of precision machinery into which so much thought and expertise has gone that you are never in danger of being sold a pup. But be wary of secondhand cameras or new models that are heavily marked down. Secondhand cameras, unless reconditioned by very reputable people, may have been sold because of some flaw such as a scratched lens, or faulty mechanism—faults which are not immediately apparent when you test it in the shop. Or some serious accident may have befallen them. Marked-down products are usually those which makers have ceased to produce for some reason, and accessories may not be available.

CHAPTER 2   Accessories

LENS HOODS OR SHADES

When I was given my first camera I was told always to take photographs with the sun behind me, because if it shone directly into the lens it would spoil the picture. It is surprising how many people think they must always aim a camera away from the sun. Of course, it is essential to keep all unwanted light—the light that is not intrinsically part of the scene—out of the lens, or halation and flare spots may ruin an otherwise perfect picture. Lens hoods, or shades as they are sometimes called, screw into the front of the lens (and will usually carry filters if necessary) and are long enough to keep out much unwanted light without cutting off the corners of the picture. They do not alter exposure readings at all. Lens hoods also protect the lens to some extent from rain, snow, spray and fingerprints.

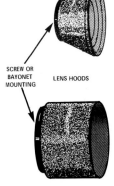

SCREW OR
BAYONET   LENS HOODS
MOUNTING

Not normally supplied as standard with cameras, though most supplementary lenses do have them, it is wise to buy a matching lens hood when you buy the camera, and to use it at all times, and you can forget where the sun is, at least in relation to whether or not it will spoil the pictures by halation and flare.

TRIPODS AND CABLE RELEASES

A tripod is very necessary if you intend to take pictures using long exposures, when the camera must be held still. It depends on how steady your hands are, but few people can be sure of holding the camera perfectly still every time for exposures longer than 1/30 th second, although if you brace yourself and the camera carefully you might manage $\frac{1}{4}$-second. Big telephoto lenses unbalance the camera and you will probably need a tripod even at 1/60 th. Use a tripod for flash photography, for then you need to be able to trigger the shutter by remote control when holding lights, flash guns, or reflectors at a distance from the camera. For sport photography a tripod is unnecessary.

Always use a cable shutter release in conjunction with a tripod. Even pressing the button on the camera by hand may jog it slightly in a time exposure.

COVERS AND BAGS

Always buy a case with the camera, unless you intend to keep and carry it in a proper padded or compartmented camera bag. To keep a camera uncased where dust can get at it, or to carry it unprotected, is asking for trouble, and spoiling the ship for a ha'porth of tar. Extra lenses, filters and exposure meters must also be kept in cases. But if you have a lot of equipment, rather than go around with it strung on straps round your neck, to bump about and get tangled up, invest in a camera bag (or gadget bag as it is often called) or a big carrying case. These are expensive items, but very necessary. Gadget bags sling round the neck, but unless well compartmented tend to get untidy. The lens you want always seems to be at the bottom of the bag, and if you are in a hurry or have nowhere to lay stuff down while you unpack it there is a risk of dropping or damaging gear. The modern attache case type of bag with foam rubber inside, which can be cut to shape or removed to take each separate item, protects cameras from damage and makes it easy to lay your hands on equipment. It is not quite so convenient as the shoulder slung bag to carry, but looks like an ordinary piece of luggage, which may have its advantages when travelling.

By the way, always put your bag of cameras on the floor of your car, not on the seat. Many a good camera has been ruined by an emergency stop which shot it off the seat on to the floor.

FILM

Film speed is always noted on the boxes in which you buy film, as either an ASA or DIN number. ASA or DIN are just different ways of calibrating speed, like Fahrenheit and Centigrade temperature calibration on thermometers. Before deciding on exposure for each picture, meter or camera (if it has a built-in meter) MUST be set to the approximate film speed number. You will find a table on your exposure meter or camera with similar numbers.

Black-and-White Film

The amateur is really concerned only with panchromatic film at various speeds, which has superseded all other types for general photography.

Type B panchromatic films are medium-speed emulsions up to 125 ASA and are so well balanced that their colour sensitivity, with a medium yellow filter, almost exactly matches that of the eye, so tones are produced at about the same level of light or darkness.

Type C panchromatic film is faster, from 200 to 800 ASA, and is highly sensitive to red and light blue, which it reproduces as very light toned indeed, needing stronger filters to counteract this.

For normal work, where speed of film is not essential, use type B film. Where you have to capture movement and where light is poor it has to be fast film. Getting movement *and* contrast at the same time by using filters will put up exposure to the point where fast film is absolutely essential, if the aperture used is to be kept small enough to give you any depth of field worth mentioning.

The slower the film the greater its power of recording detail, the greys in dark shadows and in white highlights, so that an even graduation of tone appears throughout the picture. This is linked with graininess, and slow films are fine grained in effect, so that big enlargements can be made without the definition disappearing and graininess becoming too obvious. The faster the film the more detail is lost, and the greater becomes the effect of flat contrast between black and white. At the same time graininess is increased and big enlargements lose crisp definition. This is most noticeable when using 35 mm cameras producing small format negatives. Bigger negatives, not requiring such big enlargement, do not produce such grainy pictures at the same print size.

Colour film

Colour film also has ASA and/or DIN speed ratings, which are used exactly as above when setting camera and exposure meter. The fastest colour films tend to be grainy and the colour rendering leaves something to be desired. It is only worth using them for special circumstances, where poor lighting conditions make it impossible to get good colour pictures without flash, and you do not want to use flash. Otherwise it really is a matter of personal choice. Every make of colour film differs in its renderings; some are very warm and bright, others cold and blue, others midway between. The films that have the most perfect colour rendering are not necessarily the most popular, for to many they seem to be not brilliant enough. It really is a matter of trying out films and deciding which you like best. Remember that in cloudy conditions films that tend to blueness will exaggerate the blueness of the scene and warm films will brighten it up a little, and vice versa. In snow conditions films that exaggerate blues can produce very vivid pictures. (CP. 1)

These comments apply to both colour negative film for prints and colour reversal for slides. Of course, processing is quite vital to colour films, and bad processing can spoil well-taken pictures. Even with modern machinery mistakes sometimes happen, and if you receive back work that is consistently faulty throughout a reel check with the processors. There is nothing that can be done for reserval film, but it may be possible to make better prints from colour negatives.

If you want to take colour pictures by artifical light (except flash), or at night when street lamps, etc, will appear in the picture, daylight film will reproduce the light as very yellow unless a special filter is used. To get accurate colour you must use artificial light colour film.

FLASH KITS

The old-style flash kit, in which a new bulb was needed for

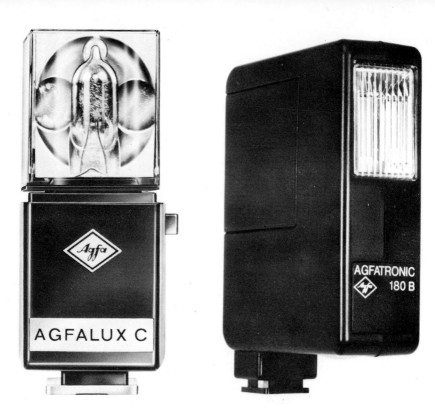

Above: A compact
capacitor unit
for flashcubes.
Powered by a 6V
battery.

Top right: Pin
electronic flash unit.
Powered by 4×1.5V
penlight batteries.

Right: A capacitor
flashgun powered by a
standard 15V battery,
and accepting capless
and AG type bulbs.

every exposure, is fast disappearing, except with very cheap cameras. Comparatively low power electronic battery-operated flash guns mounted on the camera, which provide several hundred flashes through one bulb from each set of batteries, are cheap and almost foolproof. If, however, you intend to use a flash a lot, and for subjects not immediately in front of the camera, then it will pay you to get a more powerful flash gun. These have separate wet or dry batteries in a case which slings from the shoulder, and are still small enough to mount on a miniature camera, directly, or on a bracket, without making it too unwieldly.

FLASHFLECTOR

Flash photography has problems all of its own, and one can get deeply involved with reflectors and other equipment. One cheap piece of gear that is becoming popular, where the photographer wishes to diffuse the light of the flash without losing power, is a brolly reflector. This is quite simply a white umbrella set up on a tripod with the flash gun, so that the inside of the brolly faces the subject, and the flash gun points into the heart of the brolly. The flash is then reflected back as diffused light on to the object, thus cutting down cast shadow, and reducing contrast in the eventual photograph.

Normally, cameras are set to synchronise with electronic flash at 1/60th second. There are technical problems in achieving a higher synchronised shutter speed. You will have to pay through the nose for a camera that will take electronic flash pictures at a higher speed.

INTERCHANGEABLE LENSES

Supplementary lenses for close-up work are available for most types of camera except the very cheapest, but interchangeable lenses ranging from extremely wide angle fish eye to extremely narrow angle long telephoto are not available for all cameras. As explained on page 11 various makers produce ranges of lenses which will fit their own cameras, and, sometimes with adapting rings, several standard screw threads. Some cameras have their own range. The lens is the most expensive part of

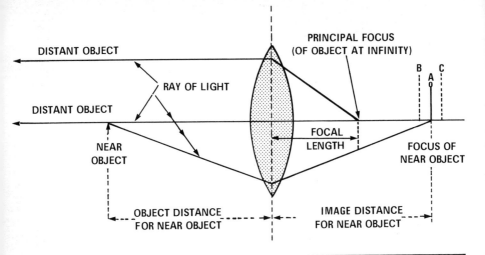

DISTANT OBJECT

PRINCIPAL FOCUS
(OF OBJECT AT INFINITY)

RAY OF LIGHT

DISTANT OBJECT

NEAR
OBJECT

FOCAL
LENGTH

FOCUS OF
NEAR OBJECT

OBJECT DISTANCE
FOR NEAR OBJECT

IMAGE DISTANCE
FOR NEAR OBJECT

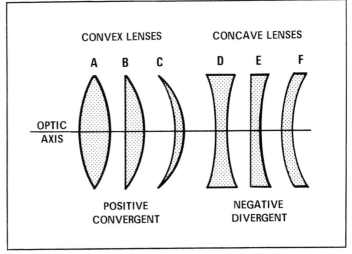

CONVEX LENSES   CONCAVE LENSES

A   B   C   D   E   F

OPTIC
AXIS

POSITIVE
CONVERGENT

NEGATIVE
DIVERGENT

any camera, and big interchangeable lenses often cost more than the basic camera.

Lenses are designated by their focal length; that is, the distance between the optical centre of the lens and the centre of the focussing screen, (in the case of the camera, the sensitive side of the film) when the lens is focussed on a very distant subject—infinity (designated 8 in photography). The focal length is engraved on the mount thus "135 mm". Lenses come in focal lengths from 8 mm to 600 mm or more.

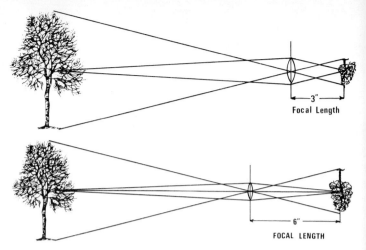

Focal Length

FOCAL LENGTH

The normal or standard lens for any camera is that with a focal length equal to, or slightly greater than, the diagonal of the negative area. Therefore, for 35 mm miniature cameras taking negatives 24 mm × 36 mm a lens designated 45 mm or 50 mm would be "normal". Twin-lens-reflex cameras taking negatives 56 mm × 56 mm have 75 mm or 80 mm lenses, and so on.

The angle of view of lenses of short focal length can be up to 100 deg, but for normal lenses is about 60 deg. A 35 mm wide-angle lens has an angle of view of about 75 deg, and this has very little obvious distortion. The effect of using such a wide angle lens is to increase the area of coverage when you are close to your subject. It is like looking down the wrong end of a pair of binoculars. Using a 35 mm lens it was possible to photograph this machinery inside a windmill from about 4 ft away. (Plate 2)

CP. 1. Winter in Austria. Although an ultra violet filter was used this photograph was taken at about 7,000 feet which in combination with the type of film that registers blues well has produced a very vivid blue picture. The ski poles and gloves in the immediate foreground give scale and depth to the picture.

CP. 2. Ski Break. Using an ultra violet filter and a 55 mm lens this was taken at f. 22 at a shutter speed of 1/60 second, to achieve enormous depth of field necessary to get both the boy and girl and the distant mountains in focus.

CP. 3. Boat-building in Spain. The large black timbers are the 'jig' in which the boat is being assembled timber by timber. All the timbers are picked out by eye by the boat builders and joined together to make the necessary curves.

CP. 4. Roof Tops of Alicante. Taken from the castle of Santa Barbara looking down on a monastery and its cloister. This is probably the only way you would be able to see over those high walls.

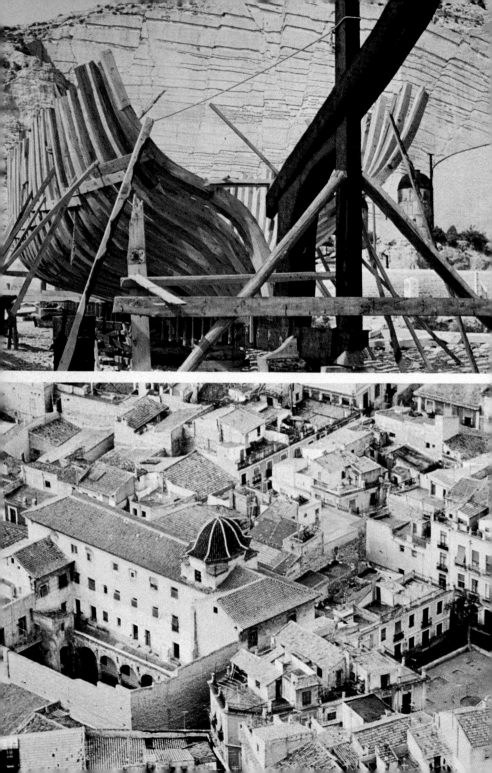

With a normal lens I would have had to step out of the window into space to get far enough back to get it all "in". When used for long shots the wide angle lens embraces huge panoramas, but everything becomes small and distant.

Telephoto lenses have the opposite effect. When used close up they bring just a small area of the scene really close to the viewer. Plate 3 was taken without the childrens' knowledge from about 20 feet away with a 135 mm lens. Detail close ups can be made of subjects too far away for standard lens. Distant views, mountain tops, etc, can be brought into close up. Of course, the bigger the lens the more "close up" the final picture will be. For photographing something small and shy, like birds, big telephoto lenses are essential, as are wide angle lenses for photographing in cramped spaces. Wide angle lenses are also useful when you want to photograph a very big subject but want to keep as near to it as possible to get good texture and detail definition. (Plate 4)

Plate 2.
The windshaft and brake wheel in the cap of a windmill. Flash photograph using a 35mm lens.

Plate 3. Concentration.

FILTERS

For normal colour photography colour filters are not necessary; in fact, colour photographs made through colour filters come out in monochrome the same colour as the filter. One has seen advertising photographs of sunset scenes over the sea, completely bathed in a level yellow light, which have been taken on colour film through a yellow filter. Ultra-violet light, invisible to the naked eye, does register as blue light on colour film, so always use ultra-violet filters (which look almost the same as plain glass, and do not increase exposure at all) in blue hazy conditions, and also at altitude, where the ultra-violet rays are much stronger because they are not being filtered out by smog and pollution as in the lower levels of air.

An UV filter used in front of black-and-white film will, especially at altitude, have to some extent the same effect as a yellow filter (below) because it cuts out blue light and therefore darkens blue areas and cuts through haze. (Plate 5)

The use of colour filters with black-and-white film is almost essential if you are to produce good photographs. In some conditions filters are not necessary (and this will be discussed in other sections of the book) but for most landscape and outdoor photography they are very useful indeed. Although modern panchromatic film produces tone values which very nearly approximate those seen by the eye, for effective photographs in black and white, which appeal to the human eye used to seeing colour, some distortion or exaggeration of tone is necessary. For instance, in most photographs taken without filters the blue parts of the sky are too light in tone, the white parts not white enough, and the grey parts not dark enough. Yellow, yellow-green and orange filters all keep some blue light out of the lens, so the blue sky comes out much darker, and the white and grey parts are lighter and darker, mainly by contrast. (Plate 5a and 5b) Heavy clouds, also giving off a lot of blue light, will likewise be darkened by a yellow filter. The blue light components of foliage, shadow, water, etc, will also be kept out and those areas darkened in proportion to the amount of blue light excluded.

Thus all colour filters affect the tone contrasts of the finished

Plate 4. Tail pole of Chillenden Post Mill. Medium film 125 ASA, f. 22 at 1/60 second, using a 35mm lens.

Note the spots of halation caused by direct sunlight shining into the lens despite the lens hood.

print by refusing to allow certain light components to reach the film. Without going into the technicalities of it any further it is useful to know what each type of filter does, (Table 1.) There are many different gradations of filter colour, but for the amateur only a few are necessary or ever likely to be used. If you have extra lenses you may want to get a set of filters for each lens, and this can mount up to quite a lot of money.

30

Colour	Effect	Factor	Remarks
Medium yellow	Passes yellow stops blue	× 2	Use for landscapes with skies and greens, slight cloud effects, seascapes. Reduces haze, increases contrasts, corrects type B Pan. film completely in daylight. (Plate 5a)
Yellow green	Passes yellow and green, stops blue	× 2½ - × 3	As above. Use also for distant views, water, snow mountains and sunset scenes, and for photography of architecture. (Plate 12)
Green	Passes green stops red and orange	× 4	Softens light contrasts, but increases colour contrasts. Lightens foliage. Use in snow and against the light. (Plate 8)
Orange	Passes red, orange and yellow. Stops blue and green	× 3½ - × 5½	Use to darken skies and water and obtain high-contrast sharp landscape pictures. Improves texture in sunlight. Good for mountain and aerial photography. Also lightens reds on roofs, buildings, etc. (Plate 5b)
Red	Passes red and orange. Stops blue and green	× 8	Darkens blue almost to black. Dramatic results when photographing light objects against the sky. Not good on greens. Cuts though haze. (Plate 9)

TABLE 2 FILTER FACTORS

Filter Factor	1.2	1.5	1.7	2	2.5	3	4	5	6	6	12	16
Open diaphragm by the following number of f-stops	$\frac{1}{3}$	$\frac{2}{3}$	$\frac{2}{3}$	1	$1\frac{1}{3}$	$1\frac{2}{3}$	2	$2\frac{1}{3}$	$2\frac{2}{3}$	3	$3\frac{1}{3}$	4

Plate 5. Distant
mountain top taken
with 135mm lens on
medium film ASA 125
using (5) a haze or
UV filter, (5a) a
yellow filter, and (5b)
an orange filter.

Roughly speaking, colour filters transmit light of their own colour and absorb light of a complementary colour. The pairings as as follows:

Red and blue green
Orange and blue
Yellow and purple blue
Green yellow and purple
Green and red purple.

Filters also reduce the total amount of light reaching the film, so, according to their colour and density, the exposure given when using a filter must be multiplied by a known filter factor which is always noted on the literature that comes with it and is sometimes engraved on the filter ring itself. The factors vary slightly according to the make of filter, but are given approximately in Table 1. This Table also gives information about the uses of filters. Table 2 gives the numbers of stops by which the diaphragm must be opened, thus increasing aperture and exposure for different filter factors.

Both Tables will be referred to in later sections of this book.

Polaroid filters almost completely eliminate surface reflections from water, so are extremely useful for photographing down into clear rivers, pools, etc.

EXPOSURE METERS
AND HOW TO USE THEM

If your camera has no meter a hand-held one is almost essential for consistently good results. By guesswork and luck pictures may come out right, but there will always be too many poor exposures. It takes years of pratice to dispense with a meter, for the true light conditions as they affect film are not at all easily judged by eye. There are times when even the experienced photographer disbelieves his exposure meter, even to the point of being sure it has gone wrong; but in fact a good modern meter seldom lics.

Photo-electric meters that register reflected light are best for general use.

The photographer sets the meter at the speed of the film he is

Plate 6. This photograph of a windmill fantail shows exactly how a white subject against a blue sky photographs using a yellow or orange filter. The whites are graduated according to the amount of sunlight upon them against a suitably darkened sky.

using (ASA or DIN) and points it at the object to be photographed. It records an average level of light over the scene if held at a distance, but if pointed directly at a dark or light part of the subject will register accordingly. When taking general scenes point the meter up and down and around all over the area and decide what the average reading is; it will probably tally with the first reading you took pointing straight ahead. But when photographing detail in a shaded area, with brighter areas surrounding it, then point the meter directly at that shaded part and expose according to the reading you get. The surrounding area will probably be slightly over-exposed,

Plate 7. Hog's Hill Mill at Icklesham. Black and white subject against a blue sky with white clouds. Fast film ASA 400. orange filter. f. 16 1/60th sec.

although the latitude of modern black-and-white film is such that it will compensate to some extent. The opposite applies when trying to photograph particularly bright areas surrounded by shadow; the exposure for the bright areas will prove to be short, so the shadowed areas will be under-exposed and lacking in detail.

Colour film has nothing like the latitude of black-and-white film, so the problems are far greater. Try taking a colour photograph in a room well lit by daylight, in which you include a view through a window to the sunlit world outside. If you set the camera to the meter reading you get from the walls,

Plate 8. Lone walker in the snow. Taken on medium film ASA 125 using a green filter at f. 22. This shows well-balanced contrasts in the snow.

Plate 9. The black mill at Barham, taken with a red filter to make the white sails show up dramatically against a darkened sky. ASA 400 on fast film.

etc, inside the room, the window area will be so over-exposed that it will come out pale and colourless, "blocked out". But if you set the camera according to the meter reading taken by pointing it directly at the window the room will come out dark and under-exposed without colour or detail, but the view through the window will be excellent! This, of course, also apples to the readings obtained with through-the-lens or built-in metering, and, to a lesser degree, when using black-and-white film.

On hand-held exposure meters the needle settles at a number on a scale, and the user then sets the same number on a marked ring on the meter at a clearly-marked point. This action rotates rings showing exposures and apertures, so that they pair up in appropriate settings for the light registered. The user can then read off the aperture (f) setting needed for the shutter speed he wants to use, or vice versa, and then sets the camera shutter speed and aperture control to match.

PROJECTORS

A very wide range of slide projectors is available for 35 mm colour transparencies. The more expensive the projector, up to a point, the better the lens will be, but one ends up paying a lot of extra money for projectors which do their own slide changing at pre-set intervals, projectors with tape-recorder plugs for synchronised tapes to describe photographs, etc.

Simple projectors take one transparency at a time, in a carrier, and the projecting lens is hand focussed by turning it manually. Another transparency is then inserted in another carrier whcih is slid in behind the lens, displacing the first transparency, and the lens is refocussed if necessary. This system is available in projectors with good lenses and the latest halogen lamps which give bright white light at a lower wattage than old-type projector bulbs. Once you have seen your slides illuminated by halogen light you will not be satisfied with any other type of lighting. This type is now standard in the more expensive magazine projectors taking square magazines holding 36 or 50 slides, or circular magazines holding

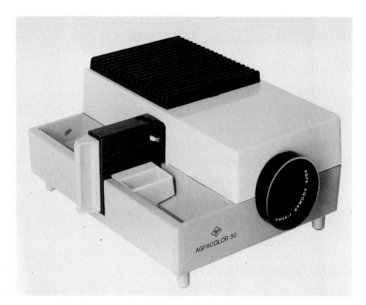

A slide projector for 35mm, Rapid, and 126 sizes. Slides rest against each other in a tray without the need for a magazine.

100 slides. Slide changing is done by pressing a button on a remote control switch.

Single-slide projectors have one enormous advantage. Slides can be kept in boxes or slide files, and selection made from there to give a show. Magazine projectors require pre-loading of slides, and this means you have no option but to show all the slides in the magazine unless you have time beforehand to set up your slides in sets, ready loaded in magazines or ready for instant loading. This can mean, if you are methodical and keep your slides properly in boxes, that you have to spend hours selecting and rejecting before giving a show. Ideally, all slides can be kept set up ready for showing in magazines; but magazines are expensive, and if you take a lot of pictures, this will add enormously to your costs.

HAND VIEWERS

BOTH BATTERY AND/OR MAINS-OPERATED.

There are several types of hand viewers, if you take many transparencies it is essential to have one with which to look at your pictures as soon as you get them, and with which to make a preliminary selection before loading magazines. One

A compact slide viewer of sturdy construction, utilizing a 75mm × 75mm magnifier lens and a 15W/240V lamp, producing a large well-lit picture. Will accept 35mm, half frame, Rapid and 4 × 4cm slides. Plus 35mm film strips.

A hand viewer for slides.

excellent type of small viewer which plugs into the mains has a carrier which takes 20 or more transparencies in a pile, and has a slide at the bottom which pushes each frame into the viewing position above a light, at the same time moving on the previous transparency into another pile on the exit side of the viewer. This is an excellent tool for quick viewing and editing, as you can run through a lot of pictures quickly and remove any slides you don't like as you go along.

NEGATIVE FILES

Loose-leaf books with pocketed, transparent pages to take negatives are most useful if you take a lot of black-and-white pictures. Negatives can be stored safely in them, and it is a simple matter to remove a page from the book, and hold it to light in order to pick out negatives. A simple system of page numbering and filing of negatives in subjects, "Boats", "Children", "Family", etc, with a check page on which numbers and subjects are listed, makes it easy to find negatives quickly.

ENLARGERS

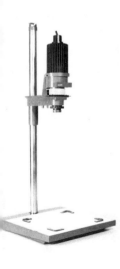

Enlargers, like cameras, come at all prices, from quite cheap to very expensive. Obviously it is stupid to use expensive cameras and cheap enlargers, because the negative is enlarged through a lens. If the enlarger lens is of poor quality then much of the advantage of using an expensive camera with a fine lens is lost. The reverse does not apply—however good the enlarger lens it won't improve a poor photograph. However, the rest of the enlarger is merely a movable lamp housing carried on a pillar, a set of condensers to spread the light of the lamp evenly over the area of the enlargement, a set of focussing bellows, including a negative carrier and an enlarging lens. The latter is the most important part of the thing, and should produce a sharp picture, when in focus, over the whole area of the enlargement, at any size.

Consult your photographic supplier and tell him the kind of work you intend to do, either black-and-white or colour, before buying an enlarger, and take his advice.

We have already discussed some of the uses of accessories—filters, lens hoods, tripods, flash, etc, as they came up in the previous chapter—but there is more to understand about using the camera before you can get planned results.

SHUTTER SPEEDS, APERTURES AND FOCUSSING

The action and use of shutter speeds is self-explanatory. The longer the shutter is open the more light it lets into the camera. But the longer the shutter is open the more time there is for the object to move and cause blurring, so it follows that shutter speeds do two things—(1) Regulate the amount of light reaching the film, and (2) regulate the amount of movement that will be apparent in the picture.

The action of the aperture, or stop control, is harder to understand. The diaphragm inside the lens, which controls the aperture, is like the iris of an eye. It makes a bigger or smaller hole, through which light can pass via the lens to the film. Therefore, if you want to take a picture of something moving so fast that it needs a shutter speed of $1/1000$ second to freeze it, but the light is poor, then the aperture will have to be opened wide to compensate—you will have to use a big stop, to get enough light to the film to expose it properly. This is simple enough to grasp. Cameras and exposure meters are so set up that normally one stop difference lets in as much more, or as much less, light as one shutter speed difference; for instance, f. 11 at $1/60$ lets in the same amount of light as f. 8 at $1/25$.

Having said all that, here comes the difficult bit! By turning the focussing ring on your camera you move the lens backwards or forwards, increasing or shortening its distance from the film at the back of the camera until the object is sharply focussed and appears to be so in your coupled viewfinder/rangefinder. Without coupled rangefinders you will have to

Plate 10. Emptying the rowing shell. A large aperture was used here so that the torso and boat are in perfect focus against an out-of-focus sea behind. Unfortunately, the legs and feet are also slightly out of focus, as they were too near the camera for the aperture of f. 4.5 which was used.

Depth of Field

Zone of sharpness increases as lens is stopped down — aperture is closed

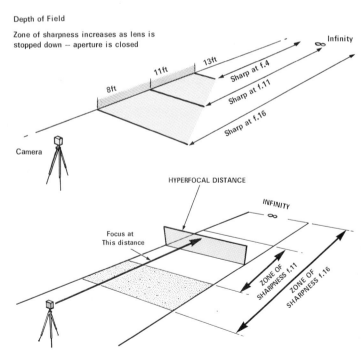

Plate 11. Skier above Innsbruck. Taken at an aperture of f. 22 the depth of field is sharp to infinity so that both horizon, some 20 miles away, and the city, 3000 feet below, are in perfect focus.

CP. 5. Cobbled Street in France. Taken when the sun was trying to break through after rain, the still-damp cobbles and stones have photographed very clearly in nice warm colours.

CP. 6. Alleyway. Taken in France, the eye travels from the beautiful colours of the stonework and pathway to the splash of sunlight just round the corner.

measure off or judge the distance of object from camera and set the focussing ring at the correct distance according to its calibrated figures either in feet or metres. Having done that accurately, whatever the aperture you are using that object will be in sharp focus on the resultant photograph. *But*, and it is a big *but*, how much is in focus, either in front of or behind the object, depends *entirely* on the aperture you use. This is known as "depth of field", and you can dramatically alter the picture by altering the depth of field. The bigger the aperture (f. 1.8, f. 2.8 up to f. 4 being big apertures), the narrower or shorter the depth of field will be. At really big apertures it is a matter of inches. Medium apertures (f. 6, f. 8, and f. 11) give a much wider or longer depth of field, and small apertures (f. 16 and f. 22) give a very long depth of field. (Plate 11).

Also, for optical reasons, the nearer the object to the camera, having focussed the lens on it, the shorter the depth of field beyond the object will be. For instance, if at f. 11 you focus on an object 30 ft away everything from 15 ft from the camera to the horizon will be in sharp focus. But if at the same stop you focus the lens on an object 8 ft away from you, sharp focussing begins at about 6 ft; up to 13 ft or so beyond the object will also be in sharp focus. (These figures vary for different lenses, but are correct for 1.8/55 mm Takumar).

Cameras which allow a choice of stops have a depth-of-field table calibrated between the focussing ring and the aperture ring. This calibration has a central red mark, on each side of which it repeats the stop numbers. Focus the camera and read off the distance shown against the stop numbers. This gives the distance on each side of the centre spot or point of focus in which the picture will be in focus. For instance, on my camera, focussed at 10 ft, at f. 16 the depth of field is shown as being from $6\frac{1}{2}$ ft to about 20 ft. Focussed at 15 ft the depth of field is from 9 ft to infinity. This may sound complex, but if you read this page with a camera in your hand it should all be quite clear!

So if your camera has a range-finder/viewfinder you should have no trouble focussing it exactly on the object and seeing at a glance how much of the picture is going to be in focus But it also works the other way, which is a great help to those whose camera does not have a depth of focus table, or who do not have a rangefinder. It is known as focussing at the hyperfocal distance. Judge the approximate distance of an object from the camera, set the focussing ring at that distance, and use a stop of f. 11. The depth of field is such, at f. 11 that unless your judgment of the distance is really hopelessly out the object will be in sharp focus in the photograph. F. 16 will give even greater latitude. Also, you now know that if you want the background to be sharp to infinity you must use the smallest stop possible, if the object is near you; and the next smallest if the object is a bit further away; and so on.

Small stop, long depth of field; big stop, short depth of field.

Having decided on the stop you want to use for focussing purposes, then adjust the shutter speed accordingly, using an exposure meter, to allow enough light to get to the film.

USING VIEWFINDERS, AND PARALLAX

One of the commonest faults of the beginner is failing to centre his subjects properly. Feet or the tops of heads get sliced off, faces peer out from the bottom of the print with large expanses of nothing behind and above them, or the subjects have apparently decided to edge sideways out of shot. And the same applies to inanimate objects; they just don't turn out to be in the right place in the photograph. This can happen even though looking through the viewfinder you saw it all exactly as you wanted it, firstly because you were not looking straight through the viewfinder, but were turning you head and squinting up, down, or sideways. To check if you are looking straight through an eye level viewfinder, move the camera a few inches directly forward; you should still be able to see the central point on which you were focussing, in the centre of the viewfinder.

The second reason for off-centre pictures is a thing called parallax. Unless viewfinders are specially corrected this can

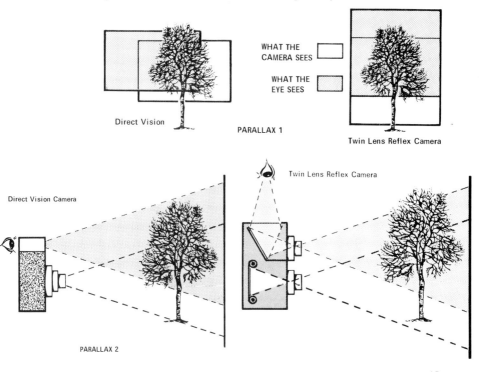

Direct Vision

WHAT THE CAMERA SEES

WHAT THE EYE SEES

PARALLAX 1

Twin Lens Reflex Camera

Direct Vision Camera

Twin Lens Reflex Camera

PARALLAX 2

45

always happen with any viewfinder that does not work through the taking lens. Simply because it is in a slightly different position relative to the subject, from the taking lens. It is easiest to understand parallax by looking at diagrams.

If the viewing lens is above the taking lens (as in a twin-lens-reflex camera), allow slightly more room at the top of the picture on the viewing screen, to avoid chopping off heads. If the viewing lens is to one side and above, as it often is on a miniature camera, then it is the bottom and right-hand side which can be cut off. You just have to learn to make that slicht adjustment. Single lens reflex cameras, with which the picture is seen through the taking lens, avoid parallax problems.

COMPOSITION

Good photographs are always well composed. Composition can be a carefully thought out thing, which has taken hours to achieve, waiting for the light to be just right, for figures to be in the right position, etc. Or it can be instinctive. Nature composes itself remarkably well, and some photographers are brilliant at spotting this. It is perhaps the mark of a good photographer that he produces well composed photographs almost without being aware of composition. He makes an automatic judgment of what he sees, either applying certain rules, or completely by instinct, or by a combination of both. "There", he thinks, "is a picture", and takes it. Later, when the result can be considered in detail, the picture probably fits most of the basic rules. The rules can be learnt, and it pays to know some of them, but without a natural eye for composition results won't be consistently good. The photographer, unlike the painter, cannot mess about to any extent with his subject, cannot leave things out, cannot alter perspectives and positions. He also has to think in terms of drastically reduced size, and inside a limited angle of vision.

The eye is a very wide-angle lens. Look straight ahead and out of the corners of your eyes you can see almost everything in front of you. Look through a view-finder and the area of vision

Plate 12. This photograph fulfils several of the rules of composition. Divide it into thirds vertically and horizontally (Rule 1) and the figures are at point C.

A	B
C	D

The composition lines intersect where the road meets the slopes of the mountains, drawing the eye, and they run more or less diagonally across the picture. (Rule 3).

The road draws the eye in from the left-hand bottom corner (Rule 6).

is strictly framed and limited. The photographers' trick of holding up the hands with thumbs touching and fingers stuck straight up to frame a picture as the camera would is a very useful quick guide to composition.

Using black-and-white film the picture has to be composed in terms of tones and not colours, so the mind has to do a translation from colour to tone, and take into account the way in which film and filters reproduce different colours as different tones. Shapes and lines and light and shade all have to be resolved into one composition.

Using colour film, the picture will much more nearly match what the eye sees, and colour masses and spots become the dominant factors in assessing composition, even light and shade

Plate 13. Beech trees. Taken on fast film ASA 400 at f. 22, using yellow-green filter, which has rendered the pale green and greys in their true tones.

being areas of differing colours, not just black, white and grey tonal differences.

Composition is a very individual thing, and varies from photographer to photographer, one being completely successful with photographs from angles with which another can do nothing. In terms of simple rules try the following:

1. Divide the picture space into thirds, vertically and horizontally with imaginary lines. Where the lines intersect, off centre towards each corner, are the best four points to place the main and subsidiary objects. Pictures with the main objects at dead centre don't seem to draw the eye, and main objects too near the edges draw the eye right off and make the picture seem very unbalanced. (Plate 12)

2. Parallel lines running across a picture draw the eye right out of it and ruin it. You can get away with parallel lines

(such as tree trunks) running up and down a picture provided
they are interrupted at some point along their length. (Plate 13)

3.   Lines that intersect at angles draw the eye to the angle,
and even if they don't intersect draw the eye to the point in the
picture where they would intersect if extended. The most
effective lines of composition run diagonally across the picture.
(Plate 12)

4.   Keep the areas of interest unequal in size. Light and dark
masses should be unequal. Never have the horizon or skyline
exactly half-way up the picture. Either keep it low down at
one third, or high up at two-thirds.

5.   The eye seeks out light, so a white or light area on a dark
background draws the eye more effectively than a dark spot
on a light background.

Plate 15. High peak. Taken with an orange filter, this picture in which dark, light and medium tones are evenly balanced is successful because composition lines run diagonally across the picture and the rock of the mountain top provides a strong focal point for the eye. ASA 125, f. 11.

6.   Try to arrange the picture so that the eye will be drawn in from one of the bottom corners. (Plate 12)

7.   People, or any object facing in a definite direction (such as a windmill) should have more space in front of them than behind them.

8.   When taking views of scenes not in close up, try to include an upright or solid object in the foreground—a tree, a rock, or perhaps a figure turned towards the distance, which will provide a darker tonal contrast, and give scale and depth to the view. (CP. 1) Pictures without an upright object in the foreground seem strangely flat, as if there is a void between the viewer and the point where the picture begins. (Plate 15)

9. When taking photographs of people, be careful that the background is not so complicated or detailed that they become lost against it. If this is unavoidable use a big aperture so that the depth of field is short and the background is out of focus, with the figure in sharp relief against it. It often pays to take figures from a low viewpoint so that heads are sharply outlined against the sky. To achieve this with a camera with an eye-level viewfinder drop down to one knee. (Plate 16)

10. Watch out for telegraph poles, flag poles, overhead wires, etc, growing out of peoples' heads. They won't be that notice-able through the viewfinder, but in the two-dimensional picture, will ruin it.

Plate 16. High pathway. Taken on fast film ASA 400 with an orange filter. The figures in semi-silhouette so close at hand enhance the sense of distance and height. See also Colour plate 1.

Plate 17. Sandwich Bay, moonlight. Taken at midday using an orange filter on fast film ASA 400 f. 22 at 1/125 sec. Overprinted to give the moonlight effect.

Plate 18. Bait-digging. Early morning picture taken directly into the light using fast film ASA 500 at f. 22 with an orange filter.

Plate 19. Rigging of the Cutty Sark. A design picture in which the eye is carried up to the cross trees although the parallel lines of the yards disobey the rules and lead the eye off the edges.

11. To imply great distances, keep horizons low.

12. Having said all this, there can be very successful pictures which ignore most of these rules; pictures which achieve a rythmic balance of objects and tone and colour masses, often almost symmetrical. This kind of photograph is extremely effective as a design, but can be monotonous. (Plate 19)

Other pictures make use of effects of light, particularly light reflected on moving water, or to silhouette objects which in themselves have interesting shapes. The amount of reflected light, or the masses of dark shadows in silhouettes, can be far greater than would be acceptable according to the above rules, but can be so impressive and interesting that you can get away with it. (Plate 18)

However the photograph has been composed when taken, much can be done to improve composition during enlarging, by reshaping the picture. If necessary, colour transparencies can be masked and rephotographed, to "crop" unwanted parts round the edges. And in black-and-white photography the trimming of the final print will very effectively alter composition.

CHAPTER 4

Photographing Leisure Activities

Now we come to the different things you may want to photograph; your leisure activities, and what better to begin with than:

HOLIDAY PHOTOGRAPHS

For the purpose of this section I will assume that you are taking colour transparencies to make a set to show your friends and to remind yourself of your holiday, although of course much of what I have to say applies also to the taking of colour positives and black-and-white pictures.

Buy film in this country; it is cheaper here than elsewhere. Always get at least two more rolls than you think you will need.

How often has one been treated to a show of holiday photographs which turned out to be just family snapshots in a different setting. "That is Mum and the kids in Venice—and that bald head hiding the gondola belongs to a man we met on the trip out. Yes, you can just see the prow of the gondola". This kind of commentary goes on endlessly. Everything you really want to see is half-hidden by people who are actually sitting in the room with you, or by uninteresting strangers, or cars. So the first rule is to take pictures which, if they include the family, have used them to enhance the picture and have not made them the centre of it. (Plate 16) Set out to take a sequence of pictures which describe the holiday and the places visited. Try to get pictures of anything unusual going on—arts, crafts, sports and work, beautiful buildings, objects and scenes not normally seen at home. As you photograph, try to find out as much as possible about the subjects, so that later on you can describe them intelligently. Then, provided the photography is technically reasonably competent, you will have your friends asking for more, rather than being politely bored.

Set the scene with one photograph of the plane or boat you travelled in, and one of your hotel or camp site. Photographs taken from high-flying aircraft or ships at sea, or out of train or car windows, are rarely very exciting, but a photograph looking down the wing of the plane as it turns to make its final landing approach can be most effective, with airfield and countryside spread out below. (Take it at f. 16 and focus on infinity to get a good depth of field, and use as fast an exposure as you can get at that setting.)

The first couple of days of a holiday are often spent on general local exploration which is a good time to get pictures of markets, harbours, local people in local costume, and general views. Markets are full of interest; piles of strange food or unusual goods; the colourful stalls in Spain which sell ceramics and copper, for instance. Photograph these things in close-up, as it is the detail that is interesting. Markets are crowded with locals, often in native costumes, but one has to be a little careful here, for many people resent having a camera pointed at them. Whenever you photograph a stranger whose language you cannot speak ask his permission by holding up your camera and smiling broadly and indicating with your free hand that you wish to take a picture. It is not hard to learn the word for "please" in any language, and that helps too. Otherwise it is safer to take photographs of people either fully engrossed in what they are doing, or of their back views, often just as photogenic as their front views. (CP. 15)

A telephoto lens comes in very useful. Using, say a 135 mm lens, you see a marvellous character about 20 yards away. Point the camera at him, focus quickly, then swing right away, with the camera still poised, and point it at something else. He will conclude that you are not interested in him and will continue with what he is doing. Then swing slowly back as if you were considering anything but him, and when he appears in the viewfinder hesitate briefly, take the picture and continue on with the swing. At 20 yards or more he will be unlikely to hear the shutter click, so will neither threaten to bash you nor try to extort a fee for having posed! In any case you should have achieved an unposed natural picture.

Scenic photographs need a foreground, or some object or person comparatively near at hand to draw the eye in the eventual picture, (Composition). Harbours and boats may be

Plate 20. Alhambra Palace. Medium film ASA 125, orange filter.

extremely colourful, but a fisherman or two in the picture will improve it. Lonely mountain views look even more lonely, and the scale is brought out if there is a figure in the right place. In Photo 12 the two figures carry the eye down the road towards the distant hills. In Photo 16 the same two figures, much closer to the camera, enhance the feeling of height and space implicit in the view. In CP. 2 the boy and girl, complete strangers to me, were resting between ski runs. The colours of their clothes were absolutely complementary to the blue and white view of distant mountains which would have been dull without them. I asked their permission to take them exactly as they were, unposed, and I think I got a winner.

See the section in this book on photographing buildings for some hints about churches, castles, etc, but always be on the lookout for alleyways, courtyards, narrow streets, preferably with one or two people in them, and where the contrasts of light and shade are good.

Local crafts made good pictures. So if there is something unusual going on don't pass by. Stop and display interest. Ask questions if you can, and after a while produce your camera. The flattery implicit in your interest should be enough to avoid the problems that might arise if you just dash up and point your camera as if they were doing something quaint or funny. The boat-building photograph, one of a sequence taken in Spain, took half-an-hour of sign language conversation to achieve, (and I learnt a lot about boat-building at the same time!) (CP. 3)

Fairs, carnivals and the like are a wonderful source of pictures, and here again a telephoto lens is extremely useful. The problem is usually that there are so many people about that it is hard to get a clear shot of what you want. Wander about and keep an eye open for the small incidents that are going on. General views of processions, dances, etc, don't convey much, although one will set the scene, but close-ups can be colourful and interesting.

There are usually far too many people in interesting buildings. I got into the Alhambra (Plate 20) when it opened early in the morning and took the shots I wanted before it became a

C.P7 Bavarian Church. Taken on a very cold grey morning with the temperature at —9° this snow scene contrasts dramatically with colour plates 1 and 2. The composition of the picture conforms to most of the applicable rules on page 47.

C.P8 The Gallery in the Chateau at Chenonceaux. Because so much natural light was coming in through the arched windows I was able to take this picture without flash. To achieve the long depth of field it was necessary to use f.22 and to hold the camera steady against a wall and use a shutter speed of 1/15 second.

crawling mass of humanity. (Also, the fact that the sun was not high increased shade and contrast.) But if you are patient there usually comes a moment when the crowds part and allow an uncluttered picture. Just a point in passing; there will always be others taking photographs and consideration for them will help you too. Try not to walk in front of another photographer just as he is about to click his shutter. And if someone is taking a group shot of his family offer to take it for him, so that he too can get into the picture. He will usually return the favour.

However impatient your family and friends may be, never pass a picture. I regret bitterly the scenes of people and things I have passed because the other passengers in my car were showing signs of edginess about stopping yet again! I remember at least a dozen of my best pictures that I took only with my mind's eye! Photographers have to be selfish.

If it is something special don't just take one picture; take several, using different viewpoints, exposures, and lenses, if you have them. The chance may never come again, and won't put your costs up more than you would happily pay for one good meal or a few extra drinks.

The final secret of good sets of holiday photographs is good editing. They may all be of interest to you, but only a proportion will be really good. So discard all the really bad pictures, however interesting, and however much it hurts—put aside all but the best two or three of any one subject—nothing bores the viewer more than too much repetition however good the pictures. Try to end up with a balanced sequence. The place, the people, the happenings, the family, mixed but preferably in the chronological order in which they were taken, so that your commentary will be smooth and informative.

PHOTOGRAPHING BUILDINGS

Many of your holiday photographs will be of buildings, or you may be interested in different kinds of buildings and architecture, from cathedrals to cottages.

The immediate problem when photographing buildings is

Plate 21. Church on Romney March. Although the use of medium film ASA 125 and a yellow filter has brought up the tones of the old stone well, the camera has been tilted backwards to get the whole subject in view, using a 55mm lens. This should have been taken with a 35mm lens to avoid the falling and tapering effect.

that they are, except small cottages, usually too big. Either too high or too long. One is forced to move so far back to get the whole subject into the frame of the viewfinder that detail is lost. Tilting the camera to get a high building into view leads only to distortion of perspective, in which the foreground and lower half of the building are exaggerated and the top narrows right off—the vertical lines not remaining vertical at all, but converging at the top of the picture, just as they do if you hold a picture flat at eye level and look along it. (Plate 21) You can

60

Plate 22. Canterbury Cathedral. Using a 35mm lens the whole great height of this scene from floor to vaulting has been included without distortion.

get away with very slight tilting of the camera if you do your own enlarging, because by tilting the enlarger in the opposite direction the lines will be brought back to true. However, too much tilting of either camera or enlarger is bound to result in distorted pictures. Architectural cameras with a back that can be tilted in relation to the lens help to avoid distortions, but are too specialist to be discussed here. For the general photographer it is best to use wide angle lenses. A 35 mm lens used with a miniature camera, be it SLR or direct view, will make

a tremendous difference to the amount of a building you can get into the picture, without causing noticeable distortion. (Plate 22) Using still wider-angle lenses may enable one to take a whole cathedral from just across the street, but the wider the lens the more the distortion or bend around the edges of the picture there will be. This bend is much the same optically as the bend you see when looking in a convex mirror, and is only acceptable for special photographic effects.

The same remarks apply to interiors. In tall cathedrals, for instance, with enormous heights from floor to vaulting. In small rooms where you cannot stand far enough back from the subject to get it all in, or where something else gets in the way, the wide-angle lens is invaluable.

Then the opposite problem arises. Way up there, out of reach unless you have a private helicopter, is some detail that can only be brought into close-up or even definitive view by using a telephoto lens. But remember once again that there will be a certain amount of distortion if the camera has been

Plate 23. Detail of a windmill. Canister and striker mechanism taken from ground level with a 135mm lens. ASA 125 film with a yellow filter.

Plate 24. Lighthouse. Fast film ASA 500 and a red filter produced this contrast of white building and dark skies.

pointed up, say at a stained glass window from floor level, so it pays to stand as far back as possible and bring the subject close with the biggest lens you own. (Plate 23)

Oddly enough, photographs taken looking down on buildings never seem to the eye to produce such noticeable distortion. Maybe it is because the roofs have patterns of their own, and lines on different planes across the picture. (CP. 4)

When taking black-and-white photographs of buildings—use medium fast, high-contrast panchromatic film. This should produce fine-grained pictures with good resolution. Use an orange filter or an orange-yellow filter to lighten brick and bring out the detail and to darken sky tones. But on the whole, unless there is to be a lot of sky in the picture which needs darkening, filters lessen the sharpness of the detail a little and need not be used. A yellow-green filter will darken sky tones sufficiently. When photographing white buildings in bright sunlight an orange filter will produce brilliant whites and dark skies, and a red filter will produce very dramatic contrasts of white and dark, (Plate 24) and at the same time cut haze to produce clear-cut pictures.

While black-and-white film records tones, shapes and details of buildings well enough when properly used, only colour can do justice to the wonderful colours of brick and stone, colour wash and red tiles. But the angle at which light is falling on the scene makes or mars pictures of buildings. High noonday light reduces contrasts and shadows. Evening light or low light are usually yellow and produce very mellow pictures. Just after rain the light is often bright and yellow and will produce vivid pictures. In stormy, changeable weather look out for wet roofs and streets shining in patchy sunlight. (CP. 5) Bright sunshine on a hot day, usually a little hazy, makes for much flatter and less interesting pictures. Little streets, alleyways and corners, preferably with one or two figures in them unconscious of the camera, photograph well, because the arrangement of lines and angles leads the eye in imagination on and out of the picture (CP. 6) Large buildings are much harder to photograph satisfactorily because these is always so much to get in the way; trees, overhead wires, cars, other buildings. Frontal pictures are not usually as interesting as pictures taken at an angle. Light falling on one face of a building will cast shadows detracting from its detail, and there is no impression of third dimension or the depth of the building. Take the photograph from an angle so that the two sides of the building can be seen. This does not necessarily apply to small buildings, little houses, churches, perhaps, which catch the eye as part of a scene. Compose the picture so that the building is slightly off-centre, and high in the picture, with the lines of the foreground leading the eye right to it. (CP. 7)

Inside buildings photography becomes more difficult because of reduced light and restrictions on camera position. It is essential to use an exposure meter, and fast film helps out. Black-and-white film rated at 400 ASA, such as Ilford HP 4, is excellent for interior photography, and in well-lit buildings you will be able to take pictures without using flash or unduly long exposures. (Plate 25) If you have a tripod exposures below 1/30 second become easy, and as filters are unnecessary

Plate 25. Monument. Taken at 1/15 second at f. 11 on fast film ASA 400 without flash, whcih has produced a much softer picture than the cast shadows of flash photography.

indoors there should not be too many problems. Flash will allow you to take interior pictures at a limited range using any film, but is no use at all for long-range subjects, inside huge cathedrals, for instance.

Use fast colour film for the same reasons. High Speed Ektachrome is perfect for indoor photography. It is fast but not grainy (some ultra-fast colour film is available but tends to produce grainy pictures in which the colour resolution leaves much to be desired) and its colour resolution is cool and well-nigh perfect, provided it is properly processed. As colour film is so much slower than fast black-and-white film it is only in very well lit buildings that it can be used without long exposures. (CP. 8) It is sometimes possible to lodge the camera against a solid surface—a pew back or pillar—but a tripod is really the answer. Trust your exposure meter, and it is surprising how the film records a picture that seems much better lit than the eye had judged it.

Plate 26. Becket Memorial. This wrought-iron memorial is off-set slightly from the wall and the use of flash in the dark church has cast a clear double image.

When using flash to photograph detail in buildings remember that it will produce very solid cast shadows from statues, relief, decoration, etc, unless lights can be set up or the flash is bounced off a white surface so that it reaches the subject indirectly. This shadow can be an advantage in bringing detail up into relief, but can produce an effect of double image in some circumstances. (Plate 26)

66

LANDSCAPE AND COUNTRYSIDE

Landscape and countryside subjects will inevitably be part of many pictures. Read the sections in this book on composition and on filters, and apply the rules to your pictures. Taking good landscape pictures is difficult. Although the eye may see a wonderful view the camera will not record it at all as the eye sees it, largely because of the enormous reduction of scale. Even in colour, long shots of landscape can be most uninteresting. The flatter the landscape the harder it is to get a good picture, (Plate 17) while mountains make things much easier. Good landscape pictures need a definite object of interest somewhere in the foreground, preferably at one of the four points mentioned in the section on composition. A house, a tree, a castle, a figure, an animal, a big rock; something to focus the picture. Plenty of cloud, provided it is not just general overcast, improves both black-and-white (provided filters are used) and colour pictures. Cloud composes itself properly because it is following wind directions down the sky, and is often dramatically lit from behind or from one side. (Plate 27)

Supplementary lenses can be useful in landscape photography. Obviously, telephoto lenses will bring distant objects nearer and narrow the angle of view, the width of the picture. Wide-angle lenses in mountainous country will give tremendous panoramic views, and used in the vertical plane make it possible to get something almost at your feet, and the summit of a mountain quite near at hand, into the same picture. But make sure that a panoramic view has plenty of interest in it, or the picture will be niggly and dull. Always look out for dramatic light effects when photographing landscape. Using a lens hood the camera can be pointed directly at the sun (although some halation spots caused by reflection inside the lenses may result if the sun is high). You can see these through the viewfinder if the camera is a single lens reflex and can place them to improve the picture. I take lots of these "contra jour" pictures, as they are called, straight into the sun, and the resultant rays of light striking earthwards have become known in the family as my "God descending" pictures. When the sun has sunk low enough to be a red disc at which you can look

with the naked eye the camera too can be pointed right at it, using your smallest aperture setting, to get those dramatic sunset pictures in colour or black and white. (Plate 28)

Reflected light on still or moving water makes good pictures. Again use a lens hood and stop down to the smaller apertures to cut out dazzle. What you are after is the spots of light, not fuzzy white areas caused by too much glare.

When photographing fast-moving water—waves, waterfalls, tumbling streams—use a very fast exposure, 1/500 second or more, and the movement will be frozen so that colours, shapes and tones come up with beautiful clarity. I rather like this. A photograph of a big wave just as it curls and breaks can be very beautiful. Or take moving water pictures a little slower, 1/125 second or 1/250 second, so that breaking foam, etc, is slightly blurred, retaining the sense of movement and force which is undoubtedly lost in the first type of picture. An exposure of 1/250 second will give you quite a bit of movement on falling or flying foam. (CP. 9)

Plate 27. Sound of Sleat. Fast film ASA ASA 500 with an orange filter against the light. This picture shows dramatically the movement of back-lit wind-blown cloud.

Plate 28. Sunset on Ibiza. Taken at f. 22 using an orange filter.

FLOWERS AND GARDENS

The glory of Britain is its gardens—suburban roses, sea-front tulips, stately homes and their parklands. Formal or informal, no other country in the world consistently produces such marvellous gardens, which just beg to be photographed in colour. But successful photography of gardens depends very much on the eye of the photographer.

Too much mixed colour, too much detail, don't make for good photographs. Look for colour masses and features such as statuary, odd-shaped bushes or rocks, or water, to build a picture around. Dark backgrounds—hedges, woods, or bushes—throw up the colour of flowers. Back lighting coming through trees can make attractive light and shade pictures. (CP. 10) Use a lens hood to reduce flare. When photographing wild flower masses, bluebells, poppies, etc, it is also important to keep the colours simple if the picture is to be effective. Use a small aperture, f. 16 or f. 22, and a slow exposure, so that the

Plate 29. Rose.

picture is in focus throughout its depth. Unless there is a lot of wind flowers are a conveniently still subject.

To photograph individual flowers, try a different technique. Use a big aperture, f. 5.6 at least, to have only the blooms you require in focus, and to achieve a dark, blurred-out background. (Plate 29) Take special care to focus the camera perfectly on the flower, and hold the camera still—use a tripod for perfect steadiness. Apple or lilac blossoms look best photographed against the sky, as the eye normally sees them. (CP. 11) Roses look best from above, preferably (and this goes for many flowers) with dew droplets on them. It may be trite, but is effective.

Black-and-white photography of gardens and flowers (although it may seem like a paradox to photograph something which is essentially colourful in black and white) can produce wonderful pictures relying entirely on the tone and composition

Plate 30. Water
Garden.

of blossom masses, reflections on water, leaves against the sky.
(Plate 30) To get good results use a medium-to-slow film for a
good range of contrasts, and filters. If the scene is predom-
inantly green, especially the light green leaves of spring, use a
yellow-green filter. This brings greens up bright and light in

Plate 31. The Lake.

Plate 32. Portrait with Flowers. Taken on medium film with a yellow filter at f. 4.5 to reduce the depth of field and blur out the background.

tone and can give the impression of translucency that you are looking for. (Plate 31) Yellow green filters also darken the sky tone. Yellow filters will darken the sky and enhance cloud contrast, but won't do much for the greens. Green filters will heighten the contrast between red blossoms and green foliage. Yellow and orange will bring up white blooms in good contrast against the sky, will darken blue flowers, but may cause some loss of the range of tone. Print flower pictures on a paper that gives warm rich tones with a wide range. A hard contrasty paper will not give such good results.

When photographing formal gardens, look hard at the design of the garden and try to make a picture that emphasises it. A photograph taken from the wrong angle may make a formal design meaningless. A high viewpoint often helps here; look down from the windows of the stately home to see the pattern of its formal garden.

Flowers go well with faces and can be used to good effect with complementary portraits. Portraits taken out of doors among flowers need care, and again a big aperture, to reduce the depth of the picture that will be in focus. But watch out for stray blooms or twigs casting shadows across the face. (Plate 32)

PHOTOGRAPHING SPORT

Motion

Every single sport involves movement, so before you can consider the problems of photographing different sports you must learn something about photographing motion.

Because you are making still photographs, not movies, the motion has to be shown symbolically. In other words, the photograph has to convey to the viewer that the subject, or parts of it, are moving. There are several ways of doing this. First, the whole thing can be frozen by using fast shutter speeds. This is fine if the shot is of footballers leaping up to head a ball, or a goalkeeper diving to make a save. The very fact that the players are in the air or outstretched convinces the viewer that they are moving. Someone running, for instance, is obviously running, he couldn't stand like that!

But take a photograph of a golfer, at the top of his swing or at the end of it, and he might just as well have been posing in that position, quite still. Take him at the bottom of the swing, when the club head is moving too fast for even high shutter speeds to freeze it, and the blurring will convince the viewer that he is actually swinging at the ball. (Plate 33) So blurring will also indicate motion. Blurring can be achieved by using slower shutter speeds, so that all movement in the picture comes out blurred. The exact definition, the detail of what is happening, will be lost, but the blurring symbolises the movement to the eye and produces a satisfactory picture.

You may want to get a picture showing clear detail of the subject, yet which symbolises motion in other ways. A moving car taken with a fast shutter speed will appear to be still. But if it is raising a cloud of dust the viewer will get the impression of motion from that. The same applies to a skier, kicking up powder snow as he makes a turn. He is frozen, but the snow proves he is in fact moving. (CP. 12)

Another way to achieve a clear picture of a moving object but at the same time to symbolise motion is to pan the camera. Imagine a motor bike racing along a road. As it passes you, you get it in the viewfinder and swing the camera "panning" with the bike. You release the shutter (using a medium speed, say 1/60 th) and in the resultant picture the motor bike will be sharply defined against a blurred background.

Obviously, the faster the movement the faster the shutter speed that will be needed to freeze or "stop" it, and by using medium speeds it is easy to achieve blurring. If something is moving at medium speed then it is very easy to freeze, and quite slow exposures will be needed to achieve blurring. I found that to blur sails of a windmill turning apparently quite fast I had to go right down to 1/15 th second. (Plate 34) In the same way something that is moving really quite slowly can be made to appear fast by using a very slow exposure to get blurring.

The angle at which an object is moving in relation to your

C.P9 Children and the Sea. Taken with a 135mm lens at f.16 at 1/250 second, the breaking wave and the sea foam make a perfect background to this holiday photo of children playing with water. The line of the breakwater carries the eye out to the breaking wave.

C.P10 Path through the trees. Taken from shade looking towards sunlight through spring beech trees with the small child in the middle distance. This makes a most successful picture.

C.P11 Pear Blossom.

C.P12 Skier. Taken with a 135mm lens at 1/500 second at f.11., a shutter speed fast enough to freeze all the movement of the skier coming directly towards the camera. The powdered snow kicked up by the skis and the balanced pose of the figure leave no doubt that he is moving very fast indeed.

C.P13 Albacore Planing. Taken with a 135mm lens at f.16 at 1/500 second, boat, figures and bow wave are frozen, but all indicate speed and movement. The balance of the figures is perfect and the light is catching the sails and hull at exactly the right angle to show the shapes and curves.

Plate 33.
Down-swing.
Taken on fast film
ASA 400 at 1/1000
second. Even this fast
shutter speed has not
'stopped' the
movement of hands or
club.

Plate 34. Majorcan
Windmill.

position also affects the shutter speeds necessary. Something
moving straight across in front of you will need a faster shutter
speed to freeze it than if it is moving diagonally across your
front. Moving straight towards you it allows the use of quite
slow shutter speeds. It is not possible to give tables for this,
because shutter speeds differ according to the speed of movement of the object, but 1/1000 th second will freeze all human
movements, though not necessarily mechanical movements.

76

1/500 second will stop most human movements. 1/250 second will probably stop diagonal movements and 1/100 second most movements towards you.

Flash and Motion

At night, or in very subdued lighting, there are several tricks you can play with motion and flash. Cameras set up for electronic flash are usually synchronised at 1/60 second. This will be too slow a speed to stop movement, and although you will get a sharp enough image, because the flash illuminates the subject for only a split second, you may also get a kind of ghost image made by the existing lighting in the room illuminating the subject for the whole 1/60 second the shutter is open. There is no way round this, except to switch off as much other light in the room as possible. Out of doors, the darker it is the better. Street lights, flood lights, etc, will give enough lighting to cause ghosting.

If you can set your camera on a tripod to take a picture of a moving object in a very subdued light against a dark background, then using flash you can make a combination picture. Take a short time exposure, and halfway through the time fire an independent flash. You will have a photograph of the object in motion across the picture, but brightly lit and sharp at one point. This takes practice and good timing to achieve.

Without special equipment picture sequences of motion can be taken with still cameras, either by working the camera as fast as you can, or by persuading the subject to repeat the action so that you can photograph it several times at different points of action.

When photographing any game played with a small ball it is very hard to freeze the ball in flight unless it is coming straight at you. (Plate 35) Balls leave bats very fast indeed, and if your trigger finger is a bit slow they often fly right out of the picture before the shutter is open. A blurred ball in an otherwise frozen shot symbolises motion very effectively. With all fast movements of this kind, or any sort of leaping or jumping or hitting action, you have to anticipate a fraction. If you wait for the exact moment you want to record, by the time your brain has told your finger to press the shutter release and the shutter has worked the moment will be past. The player will be well through the shot, the jumper will be coming down. Yet this can produce a good picture. How often has one seen a photograph of a fist thumping into a boxer's face, with the face distorted by the blow. The photographer has tried to release the shutter at the moment of impact but it is the moment just after impact that has been recorded.

Plate 35. Golf Photograph taken at 1/1000 second on fast film ASA 400. The aperture is f. 5.6 so the depth of field is short.

Whether using black-and-white or colour film, use fast film for this work. Colour film is much slower than black-and-white, unless you use the very fast colour films mentioned on page 65. Black-and-white film at 400 ASA is very useful in dull daylight conditions. And if the sun does decide to shine very brightly you may even be able to use filters to darken skies, etc, to improve the picture.

ON THE WATER

Take Care of your Camera on the Water

Seawater and sand are the camera's worst enemies, and fresh water is hardly a friend. Before taking your camera in a boat, or even to the water's edge, wipe the body all over with a soft cloth dabbed in a little silicone furniture polish. Not enough to gum up anything or make it sticky, but enough to give it a little protection. It is possible to make a temporary waterproof case with a polythene bag. Use a sandwich bag big enough to take the camera comfortably, and cut out a hole just big enough to take the back end of the lens hood. Put the lens hood on and pull the bag up to it and stick it to the hood with Sellotape. The polythene is soft enough to allow you to turn knobs and work the controls but it won't last long, and in any case condensation will build up inside it, which makes it hard to see the figures and makes the camera damp. Never keep such a bag on for more than a few hours at a time. If this expedient works for you take a supply of bags to sea with you, with holes ready-cut for various lens hoods, and a roll of tape.

Always carry a dry cloth, and wipe the camera instantly if any spray gets on it. Keep the lens cap on when not in use, and keep the camera in its own case. Always keep an UV filter on the lens to protect it from sand and sea; it will enchance the photographs anyway. Store the camera in a heavy polythene bag, tightly closed, and if you put it down in a boat be sure it is not where spray can get at it, or where it can be knocked or will fall if the boat heels. Be sure that the camera and camera bags are always attached to a line of some kind so that they cannot roll overboard. You should be wearing a lifejacket when on the sea, and it is difficult to carry a camera slung round your neck and work it with a lifejacket on, but if you are forced to take the lifejacket off keep it to hand.

If your camera or meter works by electronics or by photo-electric cells keep it away from ship's compasses or they will deviate and you may be the innocent cause of a lot of trouble.

Keep checking your lens to see if any drops of spray have got on to it, for they will cause blurring of the pictures. Keep plenty of lens tissue handy to dry up if this does happen. Watch out also for sand getting into the camera. Small children leaping around can spray water and sand over the camera before you know it. If by any mischance you do drop your camera in the water dry it as thoroughly as you can and rush it to the nearest specialist camera shop. Put exposed film away safely in water-proof containers. Tupperware boxes are excellent on small boats for camera equipment.

Dinghies

Boats are so photogenic, any boats, and none more so than sailing boats, be they fourmasters, ocean racers or dinghies. Superbly colourful, with lines of hull and sail that delight the eye. Always with surroundings of sea and sky. (Plate 36) Boats can be beautiful enough when still, masts and rigging making patterns against the sky, and hulls and sails reflected on the water. In motion they come alive, but also become much harder to photograph satisfactorily.

Racing dinghies are small boats, and helmsman and crew are always far too busy to be able to take photographs either of themselves and their boat or of others. In any case, a sailing dinghy is a dangerous place to take a camera unless it has a waterproof case. Photographs of dinghies taken from the shore or from river banks are never very exciting because the viewpoint is too high. About the most successful dinghy picture I have I got by wading waist-deep into a calm sea and persuading the helmsman to sail the boat close enough for the telephoto lens to give me a good picture. (Plate 37)

This system is fair enough for action pictures of individual boats, but normally these will have to be taken further out from the shore of sea or lake. If boats are racing you will have to get yourself into a good position and take the boats as they pass; they won't change course to come to you. The only answer is to get someone to take you out in a good steady motor boat, stable enough to allow you to stand up and move about without risking a ducking for yourself or your camera. This stable platform should be as near the water as possible; the deck of a motor cruiser with a high freeboard is again going to raise you too high above sea-level for really effective pictures.

For effective action shots of sailing dinghies, try to get positioned so that the boat approaches you diagonally. You should be to windward, so that the helmsman and crew are sitting on the side of the boat nearest the camera. Head-on shots, with crew sitting right out or trapezing, can also be effective, (CP. 13) whether the boat is close-hauled, or on a broad reach with the sails out to one side. To take a "portrait" of a boat get down to leeward and take it passing you at right angles.

Use shutter speeds fast enough to freeze the motion completely. If spray is flying some of it will probably be moving so fast that it is blurred and gives the impression of speed, but in any case frozen flying spray symbolises the motion perfectly. (CP. 14)

Plate 36. Unusually still, this fine picture of an Enterprise has a high horizon line, creating an effect of distance. (Photo Barbara Hargreaves).

With-black-and-white film, use yellow or an orange filter to darken sky and sea, bring up the clouds and whiten the sails. Remember that blue sails will also be darkened by yellow and orange filters. Remember, too, when photographing people on the deck of a boat which has coloured sails that there will be a

lot of reflected light, and on colour film faces particularly may pick up that colour reflection.

Sun direction is important. Sidelight makes lovely shadows on the sails, showing up the curves well. Light behind the camera will give brilliant colour shots, but the sails will look flatter. Light behind sails, in front of the camera, may give some fine silhouette effects, or, if the sails are thin nylon, some splendid shots of diffused light. In bright sunshine at sea trust your meter which will be giving you high readings. Failing a meter, reduce the exposure by half or one stop. (Plate 37)

Wait until the boat fills the viewfinder—the nearer it is the more impressive the shot will be. Using a small stop to get sharpness right through the picture means that exposures may have to be longer (see page 41), but generally speaking set the camera so that the depth of field extends to infinity for the stop you are using, and then use the fastest shutter speed you can without under-exposing the shot.

When taking photographs around your sailing club, wait for candid camera shots of people with their boats. Someone engrossed in doing a tricky bit of repair work on his boat will make a far better picture than he will when posed against the background of his boat in just another snapshot.

Shots of boats at different points of sailing, especially during a race, will always be of great interest to the helmsman, who can see just what he was doing wrong (or right) at that particular moment. The set of sails can be seen clearly in a photograph, taken from a viewpoint to leeward of the boat, often much better than from the limited viewpoint of the dinghy itself. (CP. 13) Photographs of spinnakers in action are particularly useful, for the sail is often hidden almost completely from the helmsman and partially from the crew.

Cruising Yachts

Any yacht big enough to walk around on provides endless photogenic subjects. Shots of sails against the sky, backlit by the sun, shots up and down the length of the boat; and, if you are agile, shots from the bowsprit and the masthead. The boat and its people, the bow wave and the surrounding sea, give

Plate 37. Sailing a minisail. That the boat is moving is expressed by the wake. The sun shines through the sail yet the boat and figures are silhouetted against the sparkling sea. Taken on fast film ASA 400 at f. 22, shutter speed 1/500 second, using a yellow filter and a lens hood.

endless opportunities. Except in foul conditions the light at sea will be good, in bright sunlight especially, so there is plenty of chance to use filters for effects on black-and-white film, and fast exposures to freeze motion with colour film. A wide-angle lens is useful for its panoramic spread from limited viewpoints. Anyone lucky enough to be able to take a camera on board an ocean racer or racing cruiser, and be allowed time off from crewing to use it, has endless opportunities for taking exciting pictures of other boats, and here, of course, the telephoto lens comes into its own.

Power Boats and Water Ski-ing (Plate 38)

Power boats are definitely not stable platforms for photography when going at speed. Even on comparatively calm lakes they

Plate 38. Power Boat Parachuting or 'Parascending'. Neither sailing nor power-boating, the man is towed just like a kite, by a power boat. Taken on medium film ASA 125, with a 135mm lens, just after take-off.

slap along in spine-jolting jerks, but by jamming and bracing yourself it is possible, using fast shutter speed, to get effective pictures of water skiers. Use a telephoto lens to bring the skier into dramatic close up. Because his speed is the same as yours, except when he swings out sideways across the wake (when is he still moving diagonally across the camera and not directly across) there are no problems about getting him sharp. (CP. 14) The slower shutter speed you use the more blurring of the wake and skier's own spray there will be, and, as with all motion photography, the more blurred the spray is the more speed it will imply. The big rear-mounted engines of power boats get in the way a bit, and it is very easy to be following the skier through the viewfinder, and to find in the resultant picture that you have also got a large lump of out-of-focus engine in one corner of it.

Nevertheless, photographing water skiers from the towing boat is really quite easy. Use a medium aperture, around f. 11, to be sure of sufficient depth of field, and a small aperture f. 16 or f. 22 to have everything in the picture sharply in focus, from just astern of the boat to the horizon.

To photograph power boats themselves in action, position yourself as low down as possible, either in another boat or on shore, and as near as possible. The same remarks apply as for the photographing of sailing dinghies, except that everything is going to happen much faster. So use fast shutter speeds to freeze the boat as it passes you and rely on the spray of the bow wave to symbolise speed. Or pan the camera with the boat, still using a fast shutter speed, so that the background is blurred. To get really effective pictures of the boats coming at you at speed you will have to find a co-operative power boat helmsman who will come to you. But watch out that he doesn't spray you and the camera with water by being over-eager. If you position yourself in front of power boats without warning you are just asking for serious trouble and inviting accidents.

Fishing
The familiar fishing picture of the angler with a grin like a proud father, holding up an enormous dead fish, is all very

Plate 39. Spinning for
Trout. ASA 500,
yellow-green filter.

well as a record of a big catch, but there are a lot of other things
to do with fishing that can be successfully photographed.

Anglers themselves fit well into landscape or seascape, and
are easy meat for the candid camera man. They are either so
engrossed that they don't see you creeping up on them, or in a
kind of trance, depending on what type of fishing they are
engaged in. They rarely smile while actually fishing, only when
the fish is landed and dead! The tension of the angler shows
well in Plate 39 trout fishing on the river Nairn, and the smile
of the victor shows well in Plate 40. The 35 lb tope in the latter
picture is far from smiling, and the enormous catch of cod in
Plate 40 are not exactly laughing their heads off!

Plate 40. The tope. Fast film ASA 400. f. 5.6, 1/500 second yellow filter.

Plate 41. Cod caught on a long-line.

Scope here for high-speed action photography of casting, and for sequence photography, from casting to striking, playing, gaffing and landing a salmon, for instance. But remember that although *you* may be able to see a fish just below the surface the camera cannot unless it is equipped with a polaroid filter.

Fishing on a bigger scale, with boats, nets, etc, provides a

Plate 42. Shark Fishing. There is a big fish on!

mass of photogenic subjects. (Plate 42) Nowadays, fishing nets are made of bright blue or green synthetic twine, which is not clearly visible to fish under water, but looks wonderful in photographs (CP. 15) and fisherman love bright colours and paint up their boats as if specially for the colour photographer!

Fishing equipment isn't particularly interesting to photograph except salmon and trout flies, which are quite beautiful in themselves, especially in colour. They present quite a photographic problem to record well. Set up against a plain white background they will look like catalogue entries. Try arranging them lightly hooked on to a cork or a piece of softwood, and photograph as close up as possible, using a big aperture so that the fly is in sharp focus against a soft background.

Underwater Photography

The steadily-increasing popularity of skin diving is also giving more people an interest in underwater photography. It isn't everyone who wants to go killing things in that serene world down there, and there is so much that is beautiful and strange just begging to be recorded on film. However, underwater photography does require special equipment and special knowledge. It is not all that difficult to make simple underwater housings for standard cameras, but there is not room in this book to give instructions for this and information about the special conditions that make underwater photography different—not difficult, but different.

There is, however, an absolutely first-class book on the subject, which gives all the information you could possibly need, both technical and artistic, and even includes a chapter on skin diving techniques. It is *How to use your Camera Underwater* by H.E. Dobbs, published by Focal Press.

GOLF

Golf is a game that requires a high degree of concentration, and even the professionals—the Jacklins and Nicklauses—who are accustomed to being surrounded by crowds and movement sometimes get upset by photographers clicking noisy shutters too near them at a crucial moment. So if you want to stay popular in the golfing world don't photograph golfers in competitions, except from a reasonable distance with a telephoto lens, and don't use flash to sharpen up a picture on a dull day; use a fast film instead.

A 135 mm lens has a wide enough angle to take a picture of a golfer with outstretched arms and club, at just about as near to him as you should be when he is playing a shot, say 20 to 25 feet. Problems that are likely to arise are that other spectators will get in front of you, or you may not be able to choose the angle you want without getting into the golfer's line of vision and distracting him, even at that distance. But to take photographs of people hitting a golf ball, for the purpose of analysing their swing, or just to make a picture, is a very different matter, and can be done effectively at a time and place on the golf course, and not during a game, when the light is right and the angles can be carefully chosen. And you can get

Plate 43. On the way down. Taken at f. 8 1/1000 second on ASA 400 with a 135 lens and a yellow filter.

Plate 44. Straight down the middle. Note the club still moving. Taken at a 1/1000 second at f. 5.6 on fast film ASA 400 with a yellow filter.

as near as you like. Using a 35 mm wide-angle lens you can stand just out of range of the swing of the club and still get in the whole action. With a normal 50 mm or 55 mm lens, from just a few feet away, the photograph will be equally effective and useful.

A golf club being swung down at a ball accelerates to such a speed that it is impossible to "stop" it absolutely by using a shutter speed of even 1/1000 second, and it is unlikely that your camera will go higher than that. Enough blurring of shaft and club head will appear on the downswing to indicate the movement, (Plate 43) and at 1/500 second you will get what looks almost like a double exposure of club shaft, head and golf ball. This blurring gives a terrific impression of power. Get fairly low down, with the camera no higher than the golfer's thighs; in fact if the photographer kneels he is just about right. (Plate 44) Try to get a clear simple background, or just plain sky, not trees or bushes.

C.P14 Water Skier. Taken with a 55mm lens at f.16 at 1/500 second. The foam of the wake and the tow rope carry the eye to the figure of the water skier and give an excellent impression of speed.

C.P15 Breton Fishermen cleaning the nets. Taken from the quay above, this back view picture in which the fishermen have unconsciously posed themselves and their nets perfectly for the photographer, was taken at f.16 at 1/25 second with a 55mm lens.

C.P16 Seagulls. Taken with a 135mm lens from the stern of a steamer at 1/500 second f.8.

A photograph taken directly in front gives the clearest view of the swing, but, especially for the drive, try standing so that you look in the same direction as the ball will travel, i.e., stand on one side of the golfer. A photograph taken as the swing ends in its follow-through also shows golf action well.

Because of the speed of movement of the swinging golfer remember to click the shutter early—to anticipate. If you wait until he hits the ball the photograph will record only the follow-through. Actually, to catch the club at point of impact is extremely difficult, and it is worth taking several pictures at different points on the down-swing to try for it. Release the shutter when the club seems to you to be halfway down to the ball.

When you show your photographs to the golfer you have been photographing, he will be very surprised, and possibly a little horrified, at what the camera shows him to be doing—but in this case the camera cannot lie.

TENNIS

The same remarks about not upsetting the players apply as they do to golf. One has seen Wimbledon players on television getting extremely edgy with photographers too near the court who are making nuisances of themselves. Tennis photographs are useful for style analysis purposes, but because tennis is a much more fluid game than golf, and the players are not in the least static, tennis photographs make fine pictures. By the very nature of the game and its players, good tennis is a wonderful combination of power and grace which photographs superbly. The photographer has slightly more time to take his pictures, as the tennis racquet is not swung with quite such force except on the serve, but on the other hand he must follow a moving player about the court and continually alter focus. The use of long lenses with their narrow angle of vision is extremely difficult, and standard or wide-angle lenses are best for the amateur, who must then pre-set the focus with a big depth of field and wait for the player to come within range. Try if possible to get the players at full stretch, whether it is for drive, volley or serve.

Plate 45. Alan Knott.
An unusual picture of
the Kent and England
wicket-keeper without
cap or pads, taken
during pre-match
practice in front of the
pavilion. The only
sort of cricketing
picture possible in
close-up unless you
have a very big lens.

Plate 46. Geoffrey
Boycott of Yorkshire
and England playing
one off the back foot.
Pre-match practice in
front of the pavilion.

CRICKET

It is difficult to photograph cricket without big telephoto lenses, because the action takes place so far away from the photographer. As it is played in good light, you can use fairly fast film and a yellow or yellow-green filter—and fast shutter speeds to get contrast between white clothes, blue sky and green turf. (Plate 45 and Plate 46)

PHOTOGRAPHING A HOBBY, OR MAKING A COLLECTION WITH A CAMERA

There are many things that cannot be acquired and taken home, but can be visited and recorded on film, to form a collection you can study at your leisure. Everything from church brasses to windmills and inn signs comes into this category, and the photographic problems will differ for each. Many of these things are inaccessible, or at any rate not near

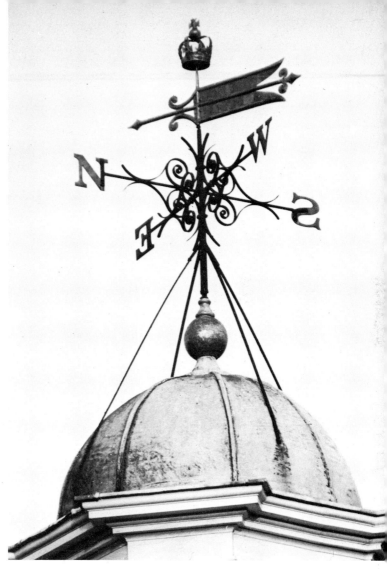

Plate 47. Weather vane. Taken with a 300mm lens from about a 100 yards away.

enough for good detail photography, and here your telephoto lens comes into its own. There is no reason why you should not make a photographic collection of cathedral vaultings high overhead, or weathervanes on steeples, using big lenses! (Plate 47)

Always take several photographs at varying exposures and from different angles. At least one or two, if not all of them, will be good pictures. Find out all you can, while on the spot, about the subjects of the photographs, and take notes either by hand or into a cassette tape recorder, which can be written up later.

If your interest is to study your collection, then black-and-white photography is the best medium. It is cheaper, and more versatile because of the wider range of film speeds. But if your collection is to be shown to others then colour slides, or at any rate some colour slides, are much more watchable. Black-and-white pictures can always be made into black-and-white slides for viewing through an ordinary colour-slide projector.

Mount your black-and-whites in an album, or in a file with transparent pockets, so that the write-up can be kept with the pictures. Put your slides into a magazine, or keep them in sequence in a box, and make a tape-recorded commentary, or a written commentary or record which matches up with the slides.

Photographic collections can provide you with a lifetime of interest, study and fun, and like many collections can begin because you have taken three or four pictures of individual examples of things in the same category which interest you, and later develop into an absorbing and fully researched study. Once I had taken my first two or three photographs of windmills, for instance, I became a collector of windmills. I now know quite a lot about them and have many pictures of windmills from countries I have visited. Before visiting new places I find out from the guide books or the specialist books on the subject where the windmills are, and tailor my trip to take in the windmills. Starting from a basic general collection of this type one can progress to detail. The sweeps or sails of windmills come in many different types, and so do other details of their mechanism, all subjects for specialist collection. (Plate 9)

I know an expert on timbering on old houses. Whenever an old house or cotage is pulled down or restored, and he hears of it, he goes along and photographs all aspects of the timbering and various types of joints, etc, taking written records of positions, etc, at the same time. Later he is able to reconstruct the building in photographic form, and to study at home the

Plate 48. Brass. Flash photograph of a rubber preparing to work on a brass. The foreshortening is inevitable, as it is impossible to get above the brass. Nevertheless it appears more or less as the eye sees it.

finer points, making comparisons with recording of other houses, and thus he has become one of the foremost experts on timbering.

Documents of all types can be photographed, and most museums and libraries will allow this if permission is asked and special appointments made. Satisfactory photographs for record purposes can be made with a hand-held 35 mm camera

Plate 49. Photographing a big brass rubbing. Nearly eleven feet long, the problems are apparent in this photograph, particularly that of getting the subject evenly lit. Taken with a 35 mm lens, with the camera on a tripod, and focussed very carefully. To make a print of the rubbing itself only that part of the negative would be enlarged.

using a standard 50 mm lens, but if much work has to done it is easier to set the camera on a tripod and pin the material to be copied to a board set absolutely level in front of it. Focussing can then be very exact. However, to get close enough to documents with small script to photograph them properly it is necessary to use extension bellows, which fit between lens and camera body, and make it possible to focus the lens on objects very close to it. This is specialist work beyond the scope of this book, but is detailed in most technical books about photography.

Photographing small objects for record purposes, such as coins or medals, is a matter of lighting. To show up very low relief, set a bright lamp very low to one side of the coin, and

Plate 50. Brass rubbing.

another much weaker one on the other side to soften the cast shadow. In the photograph the cast shadow will show up the relief. Be careful not to place the lights so that the shadows become elongated and distort the shapes. Practice makes perfect.

I have spent much time photographing monumental brasses in churches. A difficult subject, because ideally one should be directly above them, and to get high enough over a twelve-foot brass you need scaffolding or a sky hook! But even by climbing on a chair or a pair of steps one gets up high enough to reduce the angle sufficiently so that the foreshortening is not too bad. (Plate 48) And as it is usually necessary to use flash, both to get enough light, and to bring up the engraving by means of cast shadows, be careful that the flash does not reflect straight back into the camera from the brass, making a bright area which will be difficult to print up to show detail. In well-lit churches it may be possible to get good pictures with time exposures, the camera being set on a tripod. But unless there is enough light to cast slight shadows the picture will inevitably be flat.

A wide-angle lens about 35 mm is very useful for big brasses.

To photograph brass rubbings on white paper it is essential to have the rubbing evenly lit. Hard to achieve except out of doors on a calm day. Try sticking the rubbing to a picture window, on its side if necessary, (Plate 49) and again use a wide-angle lens, with the camera on a tripod so that you can get very exact focussing. Use slow black-and-white film to achieve contrast pictures, and print on to hard contrasty paper. (Plate 50)

BIRDS

To photograph birds from hides on nature reserves, etc. is a job requiring masses of patience and time, and expensive long lenses. But if you are really interested in birds and have a garden it is surprising how many species, even in a town, will come to a bird table; 20 or more. So first of all you must set up a bird table conveniently within range, 4 to 10 feet, of a house or shed

Plate 51. Wild Geese coming to be hand-fed, taken with a 135mm telephoto lens.

window which is preferably open, but certainly absolutely clean. Provide the appropriate food for the species you want to attract, and make use of their special preferences to set up photographs. Most birds like to perch near a bird table before they fly to it, to make sure everything is in order—no lurking cats, or bigger birds that may bully them. It is this need to perch that gives one a chance to set up a photograph. A conveniently-placed twig or bough can be attached to the bird table itself, or to stakes that can be moved around. Having provided a nice branch or log as a perch sit back and watch the birds. If they don't use it, it may be too high or too low, or not in the line of flight they like. Move it around or set out several perches until the birds have declared their preference. A bird bath also provides an excellent point at which to photograph, and again you can move this around until it is in a good position photographically.

Make a curtain with a slit in it for a shed window. House curtains can be held together with clothes pegs or bulldog clips to leave a hole just big enough to get the lens through. Set the camera up on a tripod (and flash if you are using it) and pre-set the focus as nearly as possible. Use a medium

98

aperture to blur out the background and produce a sharp picture of the bird, but don't try for an aperture so big that the depth of field will be less than the length of the bird from head to tail, or the result will not be good. Be ready to adjust the focus once the bird has alighted: f. 11 or f. 16 at close range, 4 to 8 feet, will give enough depth without sharpening the background too much. A 135 mm lens will give excellent results, set up to focus as close as it will; and you won't have to get much further back even with bigger lenses. No bird bigger than a thrush is likely to come to your table, but if one does, chase it away before it frightens off all the small birds for good.

Electronic flash will, because it is fast, stop most movement. The problem here is that most SLR cameras will only take electronic flash at a shutter speed of 1/60 second, and if there is any amount of normal lighting, even dull daylight, the film will record movement, even though the flash itself is fast. Also, if you are as close to the subject as suggested above, either a faster shutter speed or a small aperture, probably a combination of both, will be necessary to avoid over-exposure. But the small aperture will allow all the background detail to be in focus and complicate the picture. So when using flash it is best to arrange your perches so that the bird will be far enough away from the camera, at least 10 feet, to allow a medium stop to be used without over-exposure. This is where it pays to use a longer lens to bring the bird back into close up. If possible, open the window so that there is no chance of the flash reflecting back in the glass.

If you do have a camera which can synchronise flash pictures at fast shutter speeds it is ideal for this work, as you can stay close to the subject, stop movement, and use a big enough aperture to blur out the background, and still not over-expose.

Extend these principles to photography from hides. The hides set up for photographers on bird sanctuaries force you to wait until a bird arrives to be photographed, but you may find a nest or a feeding or drinking place where you could set up a hide for yourself. Obviously it is best to make a hide of materials that blend fairly well into the background, but birds are not unduly disturbed by a hide once they have got used to it,

Plate 52. Sing. 1/500
second at f. 4.5 on
ASA 125 film.

and if you get into it quietly and stay put without noise they will eventually return to be photographed. I have heard it said that if two people enter a hide and after a few minutes one leaves it and goes away the birds, which can't count, imagine it to be empty and will therefore ignore it completely.

It is extremely difficult to photograph wild birds on the wing, or without being able to conceal oneself. Long lenses help a bit with bigger birds such as duck, or comparatively tame birds, but one is lucky indeed to get near enough to the shyer birds to take a photograph worth having. (Plate 16)

On one occasion, driving in my car, I saw a skein of greylag geese coming in from the sea a couple of hundred feet up. I got carefully out of my car (there were several other cars, moving and parked, nearby) and stood beside it. I pointed the camera (with a 135 lens on) up at the geese and instantly

Plate 53. Tam with roses.

Flash photograph; note how wide the pupils of the cat's eyes are. The room was not very well lit, but the flash is much too quick to cause the pupils to contract.

the skein broke and jinked up and away from me. I checked with the sun angle and realised that my lens must have heliographed a flash of light (perhaps they imagined it was a gun shot) straight at them. So the picture I got had neither form nor close-up detail, and you must have one or the other or both.

PETS

If there is one thing that takes endless patience it is photographing pets. When your dog, cat, cat, otter, gerbil, guinea pig, budgerigar or whatever poses itself perfectly or does something really interesting you just never happen to have the camera to hand. Although a cat may have been asleep for hours in a patch of sunlight I guarantee that if you go to fetch a camera she will have wakened up and disappeared by the time you get back!

Self-posed animals rarely choose simple backgrounds. The plain light or dark background which shows up the creature at its best is hard to achieve except in studio conditions against screens—and then the animal usually decides that it is totally uninterested in watching the birdie or anything else and goes to sleep.

Cats and dogs will at least stay still in one place for long enough to have their portraits taken, (Plate 52) and the background problem can be overcome by using a big stop, not more than f. 4, and thus a short depth of field and a soft background. Get as close to the animal as focussing the camera will allow.

When photographing animals in movement—a cat jumping, or a dog catching a ball—remember to press the shutter, set at a high speed, at the instant before the top of the jump, so that the animal is still going up, or at any rate not coming down, on the photograph.

Cats go well with flowers, and quite obviously enjoy their smell. (Plate 53) A cat photographed among flowers in a garden, or with a vase of flowers indoors, always looks completely "right". But cats do seem to have a natural ability to pose, and are among the most rewarding of animals to photograph.

Photographing animals out of doors is best done with a telephoto lens, as one can rarely get near enough to the subject, especially if it is on the move. Pointing the camera sharply down from ones own eye level will produce a lot of distortion, large-headed dogs with long tongues leering up at you above tiny bodies and short legs. There is always the problem of getting down to the same level as the animal, or contrariwise, getting the animal up to the same level as the camera. Photograph it on a mound or a wall or a bank.

HORSES

Because horses are much taller than you, and the eye-level camera will be somewhere around the same level as the horse's nose, they are much easier to photograph than are small animals. To photograph horses in motion—racing or jumping— apply the techniques described in the section on motion photography. The positions of the horse's legs, and of the rider, will be frozen in a detailed photograph taken at fast shutter speed, and will thus give plenty of speed symbolism. Blurring,

at slow shutter speeds with the camera held still, will probably not give the result you want, for too much detail will be lost. The third method, panning the camera at the same speed as the moving animal and using a medium shutter speed, photographing it as it goes by, will produce fine sharp pictures against a blurred background. Again, remember to release the shutter fractionally before the subject reaches the point you want. Get as close to, and as well under, jumps as you can or dare; sit on the ground and photograph upwards. To photograph a race coming towards you, use a wide angle lens from the rails to get the whole lot in picture, then enlarge the result to trim out unwanted foreground, etc. To get an impressive picture of a single horse racing towards you, use a telephoto lens and take it as near as you dare. At the races, photograph the near-side horse from the rails; duck back in time, though!

The position of a galloping horse's legs in a photograph will make a difference to the impression of speed, but the movements are so quick that it is almost impossible deliberately to take a selected leg position, so take several pictures.

To take a photograph of a horse standing still, the horse being a long animal, it should be posed at right angles to the camera if foreshortening is to be avoided. (Plate 54) Make sure that the horse is standing correctly, with all four legs straight, the back legs reaching backwards just a little and the front legs more or less square with each other. This applies whether the horse is being ridden or not. A slight turn of the horse's head towards the camera is good. Horses can look very dopey in photographs. It will be best of all if something just behind you can catch their interest so that their ears prick and eyes open wide. Someone waving a handkerchief at the right moment can help, but be careful not to frighten the horse too much!

STUDYING THE WEATHER WITH A CAMERA

Colour film records skies so beautifully that one can get carried away and spend an awful lot of film on clouds and sunsets. Yet when photographing other things one is never specially conscious of the meteorological significance of the sky behind. Next time you are projecting slides take time to study the skies and think back on how the weather developed during the next 12 hours or so after the picture was taken. Several simple books on weather are available. The one in the Observer range is excellent. They will help you to recognise the typical cloud formations, etc. With a little thought and study you can become quite a weather forecaster. Not only cloud formations, but mist and haze lying at different levels, and excessively clear conditions, can be photographed and all have a bearing on the weather. Photograph unusual cloud formations or types, for study and comparison later. (Plate 55 and 55a)

To make a serious study of meteorology, photographs should

Plate 55 and 55a.
Storm clouds building
up at sunset.

be combined with records of temperature, windspeeds and directions, rainfall, humidity, and barometric pressure. Build up a whole set of photographs of different meteorological phenomena, from rainbows to dew, from lightning to hoar frost, to back up an interesting hobby, and the end result will probably be a fascinating collection of nature pictures.

It takes good luck to get lightning pictures. First you need a heavy storm at night. Next a good viewpoint, preferably under cover, where the camera can be set up on a tripod.

There must be no street lamps, car headlights or lights from windows to spoil the picture. Use your smallest aperture; and point the camera at where you think the next flash will happen. Set the focussing ring at infinity. Set the shutter speed control for time exposure. Use a cable shutter release. Open the shutter, and wait for the next flash of lightning. As soon as it has happened, close the shutter. The luck is in having the camera pointing in the right direction and in getting a good flash far enough away to register mostly as lines of light, with not too much general flare.

In this book I have tried to cover the basic knowledge required of the beginner, and I hope that it will whet the appetite of the potential photographer and help newcomers to this fascinating hobby.